YOUR FIRST INTERVIEW

For Students and Anyone Preparing to Enter
Today's Tough Job Market

By

Ron Fry

CAREER
PRESS

The Career Press, Inc.
Franklin Lakes, NJ

Your First Interview

Edited and typeset by Nicole DeFelice

Cover design by Johnson Design

Printed in the U.S.A. by Book-mart Press

To order this title, please call toll-free 1-800-CAREER-1 (NJ and Canada:201-848-0310) to order using VISA or MasterCard, or for further information on books from Career Press.

CAREER PRESS

The Career Press, Inc., 3 Tice Road, PO Box 687,
Franklin Lakes, NJ 07417
www.careerpress.com

Library of Congress Cataloging-in-Publication Data

Fry, Ronald W.
    Your first interview : for students and anyone preparing to enter today's tough job
    market / by Ron Fry.—4th ed.
        p. cm.
    Includes index.
    ISBN 1-56414-586-7 (paper)
        1. Employment interviewing. I. Title.

HF5549.5.I6 F76 2002
650.14—dc21   2001059872

Contents

Introduction

The Interview Process, in Good Times and Bad

Unemployment is at a record high...or record low.

Jobs are plentiful...or scarcer than lilacs in December.

We're at war...or peace.

And you've got a job interview, your *first* job interview, which is happening whichever of the above scenarios occur. To be truthful, they aren't as important as you probably believe. Whether the economy is coasting down Easy Street or preparing to nosedive off the Wall Street pier has little to do with how you land your first interview, prepare for it, conduct yourself during it, and whether you emerge successfully from it...with your first job in hand.

So don't worry if the papers are full of doom and gloom, trumpeting the worst job market for college grads since the reign of George III. And don't get too cocky when the business magazines tell you "It's a Seller's Market!" and visions of six-figure starting salaries start dancing in your head. Whatever circumstances you face, it's still your first interview, and you are probably scared stiff.

They *can* spot you a mile away

Most hiring managers and recruiters have little trouble identifying candidates who are waiting for their first interviews.

There they sit in the reception area, those impeccably dressed collegians in standard-issue interview suits.

The nervous *thump-thump-thump* of their hearts is almost audible.

They all seem afflicted with Lady Macbeth Syndrome, constantly rubbing their palms on their thighs in hopes of drying them before they have to shake the interviewer's hand.

There *are* plenty of good reasons for you to be nervous. You are faced with the task of convincing a total stranger to invest company money and time in *you*. Indeed, selling yourself in a competitive market is a daunting task.

And despite what I said just a few paragraphs ago, the situation as I write this is pretty darned dire—the remnants of the dotcom bust are still smoldering, Wall Street is in free fall, consumer confidence is somewhere between slim and none, and most of us have yet to recover from 9-11.

And you're more likely to contend with a tougher interview than your slightly older friends because of the rapidly increasing sophistication of those doing the hiring for America's companies. Corporations are spending more money than ever on psychological tests, honesty tests, drug tests, assessments, and computerized screening systems.

They are sending recruiters and supervisors to courses on interviewing and candidate-evaluation procedures. They are subjecting candidates to more and longer interviews.

And they are using new interviewing techniques, some of which would make thumbscrews seem like an attractive alternative.

Although it would be unrealistic to expect any new hire to come with a guarantee, many employers are taking that extra step to make sure they do not even *consider* someone they will quickly wish had never darkened their doors. Simply put, employers can afford to be choosy, and they've found better ways to choose. They are seeking "self-managing" employees— young people who are versatile, confident, and not afraid to roll up their sleeves and get the job done.

But you can't prove you're exactly what they're looking for without making it through the interview process.

If you haven't taken a lot of time to uncover the "real you" beneath the grades and athletics and clubs, don't worry. By the time you finish today's interview process, you'll be ready to lead a self-help seminar on "Getting in Touch With Your Inner Child."

Help is in your hands

But the purpose of this book is to ease your anxiety, not add to it.

Of course, the best way to keep anxiety from hamstringing you during the interview is to be thoroughly prepared. Know yourself. Know the company. And, if possible, know the interviewer. *Before* you're sitting in the reception area filling out an application.

This book will help you do that. It will also help you write effective letters that will get you in the door to show your stuff. It will give you a sneak preview of exactly what to expect during the interview. It will even tell you what your "interview suit" should look like.

Most importantly, this book will tell you, in detail, how to conduct yourself during every phase of the interview—how to make sure you're taking the right approach once you get to know the interviewer a bit, and what you can expect to be asked.

It will tell you how to handle illegal or embarrassing questions, how to field the job offer, and how to make the most of salary discussions.

Like playing the piano, interviewing takes practice. And practice makes perfect. Hours of personal interviewing experience—the tragedies and the triumphs—as well as my years as an interviewer are the basis for this book. My intention is to spare you many of the indignities I suffered along the way by helping you prepare for the interview of your worst nightmares—at a comfortable distance from the interviewer's glare.

You *can* take charge

Most of the advice in this book is pure common sense. But even the most seasoned job hunters who read it might well ask, "Why didn't *I* think of that?"

The reason is simple: Most job candidates misunderstand their role in the process. They think of the interview as an interrogation. And they see themselves as suspects, not as the key prospects they really are.

This book will show you that *you* are, to a very large degree, in charge of the interview. It will convince you that you are there not only to sell the company on *you*, but to make sure that you are sold on *the company*.

Simply put, the interview is not a police lineup—it's a two-way street.

What's the worst that can happen?

As you ready yourself for any particularly stressful situation—an important exam, a big date, *your first interview*—it's helpful to put things in perspective by asking, "Well, what's the worst that can happen?" Here are some true life stories you won't believe:

- One candidate, who was extremely nervous at the start of the interview, reached across the interviewer's desk to deliver his resume and split his suit jacket wide open, explaining, "I knew Dad's clothes didn't quite fit."

- One man continually asked the director of human resources if he could phone his psychiatrist to make sure he was answering the questions correctly.

- A candidate at one company laid down on the floor through the entire interview, taking the hiring manager's advice to "relax" perhaps too literally.

If you're well prepared—and relatively sane—it's unlikely that any of these mishaps will befall you. Preparation is the key to surviving the interview process. Just follow the advice in this book and you're sure to be one of the best candidates that interviewer has ever seen. So don't worry. Read on!

Chapter 1

How to Develop Your Personal Inventory

What constantly surprises many interviewers about first-time job seekers is how unprepared they are. These professionals tell me that too many inexperienced job seekers think they can just "wing it," and that the majority of them usually end up tongue-tied when asked the simplest questions…the ones they should know are coming.

You may have mailed a gorgeous resume and cover letter. You may be wearing the perfect clothes on the day of the interview. But if you *can't* convince the interviewer—face-to-face—that you are the right person for the job, you *aren't* getting hired.

Too many candidates hesitate after the first open-ended question, then stumble and stutter their way through a disjointed litany of resume "sound bites." Other interviewees recite canned replies that only highlight their memory skills.

For example, the most common job interview question of all time—"So, tell me about yourself."—hits most first-time job seekers like a stun gun. A typical candidate searches her brain frantically for the right answer to this seemingly innocuous question.

This common interview question is not at all innocuous. It can make or break the job interview. As a job candidate, you should view this question as a wonderful opportunity to sell yourself to a prospective employer. It may be the only time during the whole job-hunting process that you can talk freely, highlighting those very things that make you uniquely qualified for employment.

Unfortunately, most candidates wind up hemming and hawing and growing more and more nervous until they end up knocking a chair over on the way out. Memorable exit—no job.

So, tell me, who are you?

The object of this chapter is to prepare you to comfortably answer one—and *only* one—question: "Who are you?" The success or failure of many interviews will hinge on your ability to answer this seemingly simple question.

The interviewing process is a kind of sale. In this case, *you* are the product—and the salesperson. If you show up unprepared to talk about your unique features and benefits, you're not likely to motivate an interviewer to "buy." Most candidates don't really have an answer for, "How would you describe yourself?" or, more simply, "Who are you?"

They don't know the answer because they've probably never *really* thought about the question. Most people are uncomfortable with introspection. And let's face it, the days immediately before and after graduation seem like the wrong time for contemplating your navel.

However, it's essential to take the time now to get to know yourself better. You might have soared through school with flying colors, but you'll spiral out of the job market unless you take the time to perform a personal inventory.

There are decidedly selfish reasons you should do so. In the course of your lifetime, you'll work some 60,000 hours. Whether that work is productive and fulfilling will depend to a large extent on how well you've identified and utilized your dominant skills and talents, right from the start. Correctly match your skills and talents with the right industry, job, and company, and your work life will be a successful and happy one. If you don't, you'll wind up frustrated, unhappy, and unfulfilled. Given a choice, I recommend the former!

Information at your fingertips

Have you put together a resume?

Of course you have. Well, that process should have provided all of the information you need to answer the question, "Who are you?" in a way that will knock the interviewer's socks off. Most candidates go about putting together a resume as if it were merely a catalog of their accomplishments and education. A resume should also be a reflection of the "real you" behind the facts and dates.

You must look at the process of putting together your resume as a chance to examine those qualities that make you special and those you'd like to improve. It is also an opportunity to organize a great deal of information about your education, the jobs you've held, and your volunteer activities.

How you should put together a resume is discussed at length in the companion volume to this book, *Your First Resume, 5th Ed*. Here's a brief look at the process.

You need to assemble all of the following information. Keeping separate folders with pertinent data, citations, notes, etc., is an excellent idea.

Your employment history

Prepare a separate sheet for every full-time and part-time job you've ever held, no matter how short the tenure. Yes, even summer jobs are important here: they demonstrate resourcefulness, responsibility, and initiative—that you were already developing a sense of independence while you were still living at home. Whether you choose to include some, all, or none of these short-term jobs on your resume or to discuss them during your interview is a decision you'll make later. For now, write down everything about *every* job. For each employer, include:

- Name, address, and telephone number of the company (plus an e-mail address if you have one).
- The names of all of your supervisors and, whenever possible, where or how they can be reached.
- Letters of recommendation (especially if they *can't* be reached).
- The exact dates (month and year) you were employed.

For each job, include:

- Specific duties and responsibilities.
- Supervisory experience (the number of people you managed).
- Specific skills required for the job.
- Key accomplishments.

- The dates you received promotions.
- Any awards, honors, and special recognition you received.

For each part-time job, also include:

- The number of hours you worked per week.

Don't write a *book* on each job. Concentrate on providing *specific data* (volume of work handled, problems solved, dollars saved) to paint a *detailed* picture of your abilities and accomplishments. Believe me, these hard facts will add a powerful punch to your interview presentation. For example:

- Duties: Write one or two sentences giving an overview of the tasks you handled in each of the jobs you held. Use numbers as often as possible to demonstrate the scope of your responsibilities.
- Skills: Name the specific skills required to perform your duties—highlighting those that you developed on the job.
- Key accomplishments: This is the place to "brag." But be sure to back up each accomplishment with specifics, including results.

Your volunteer activities

The fact that you weren't paid for a specific job—such as stuffing envelopes for a local political candidate, running a car wash to raise money for the homeless or manning a drug hotline—is no reason to leave it off your resume. Having hired hundreds of people during my career, I can assure you that your "after-hours" activities will be considered and weighed by many interviewers. Workaholics rarely make the best employees.

So take some time to make a detailed record of your volunteer pursuits, similar to the one you've just completed for each job you held. For each volunteer organization, include:

- ◆ Name, address, and telephone number (plus e-mail address, if available).
- ◆ The name of your supervisor or the director of the organization.
- ◆ Letter(s) of recommendation.
- ◆ The exact dates (month and year) of your involvement with the organization.

For each volunteer experience, include:

- ◆ The approximate number of hours you devoted to the activity each month.
- ◆ Specific duties and responsibilities.
- ◆ Specific skills required.
- ◆ Accomplishments.
- ◆ Any awards, honors, and special recognition you received.

Your educational accomplishments

If you're a recent college graduate or still in college, you don't need to rehash your high school experiences. If you have a graduate degree or are a graduate student, however, you should list both graduate and undergraduate course work. If you're still in school and graduation is more than a year away, indicate the number of credits you've earned through the most recent semester completed.

Your extracurricular activities

I'm always interested in—and impressed by—candidates who talk about books they've read and activities they enjoy. So make a list of all the sports, clubs, and other activities in which you've participated, inside or outside of school. For each activity, club, or group, include:

- ◆ Name and purpose.
- ◆ Any offices you held; special committees you formed, chaired or participated in; or specific positions you played.
- ◆ Duties and responsibilities of each role.
- ◆ Key accomplishments.
- ◆ Any awards or honors you received.

Honors and awards you've received

List all the awards and honors you've received from school(s), community groups, church groups, clubs, and so on. You may include awards from prestigious high schools (prep schools or professional schools) even if you're in graduate school or long out of college.

Your military record

Many employers are impressed by the maturity of candidates who have served in the armed forces and consider military service excellent management training for many civilian jobs. So if you've served in the armed forces, even for a short time, make sure you can discuss your experiences and how they mesh with your professional aspirations. Be sure to include:

- Final rank awarded.
- Duties and responsibilities.
- Citations and awards.
- Details on specific training and/or any special schooling.
- Special skills developed.
- Key accomplishments.

Languages in which you're fluent

Even if you're not applying for a job in the international arena, your ability to read, write, and/or speak a second language can make you invaluable to employers in an increasing number of research and educational institutions or multinational companies. One year of college Russian won't cut it. But if you spent a year studying in Moscow—and can carry on a conversation like a native—by all means write it down.

At the end of this chapter, I have included 10 data input sheets. The first eight cover employment, volunteer work, education (4), activities, and awards. The last two—which cover military service and language skills—are important if, of course, they apply to you.

While you should use these forms to summarize all the data you have collected, do not throw away any of the specific information—report cards, transcripts, citations—just because it's recorded on these worksheets. Keep all your records in your files. After all, you never know when you might need them again!

Dig a little deeper

Once you fill in these forms, you'll see that they contain a great deal of information. But all they really reveal about you is what you've done and where you've been. These facts alone will not ordinarily land you a job. You must take some time to think over your personal history so that you will be prepared to present the "real you" during the interview. Use the following questions as a guide:

1. Which achievements did you enjoy most? Which are you proudest of? (Be ready to tell the interviewer how these accomplishments relate to the position at hand.)

2. What mistakes have you made? Why did they occur? How have you learned from them? What have you done to keep similar things from reoccurring?

3. How well do you interact with authority figures—bosses, teachers, parents?

4. What are your favorite games and sports? Think about the way you play these games and what that says about you. Are you overly competitive? Do you give up too easily? Are you a good loser—or a bad winner? Do you rise to a challenge or back away from it?

5. What kinds of people are your friends? Do you associate only with people who are very similar to you? Do you enjoy differences in others—or merely tolerate them? What are some things that have caused you to end friendships? What does this say about you?

6. If you were to ask a group of friends and acquaintances to describe you, what adjectives would they use? List all of them—the good and the bad. Why would people describe you this way? Are there specific behaviors, skills, achievements, or failures that seem to identify you in the eyes of others? What are they?

This exercise will be most effective if you write down your answers. Because it's for your eyes only, you needn't be concerned about producing beautiful prose, or, for that matter, even complete sentences. The only important thing is honesty.

Painting the whole picture

Now, look over all that you've written down so far and distill it into several lists with the following headings:

- My strongest skills.
- Areas in which I am most knowledgeable.
- Strongest parts of my personality.
- Things I do best.
- Skills that I should develop to do well in my career.
- Parts of my personality I could stand to improve.

If you take the time to do this exercise honestly and thoroughly, you will be amazed at the results. It should help you realize things about yourself that you never knew or, more accurately, that you never *knew* you knew.

I urge you to engage in this process of self-examination, even if there is no imminent need to use the information. Then, when you set up your first interview, take out your lists, along with another clean sheet of paper, and answer the following questions:

1. What in my personal inventory will convince this employer that I deserve the position for which I'm going interviewing?

2. What are the strengths, achievements, skills, and areas of knowledge that make me most qualified for this position? What in my background should separate me from the pack of candidates for the position?

3. What weaknesses should I admit to, if asked about them, and how will I indicate that I have improved or will improve them?

I hope that this first chapter has convinced you of the importance of doing your homework before the interview. If not, the next few chapters will demonstrate just how essential that homework will be.

Employment Data Input Sheet

Employer Name: _____

Address: _____

_____

_____

Phone: _____

E-mail: _____

Dates of Employment:_____to _____

Hours Per Week:_____ Salary/Pay: _____

Supervisor's Name & Title: _____

Duties: _____

_____

_____

_____

_____

Skills Utilized: _____

_____

_____

_____

_____

Accomplishments/Honors/Awards: _____

_____

_____

Other Important Information: _____

_____

Volunteer Work Data Input Sheet

Organization Name: _____

Address: _____

_____

_____

Phone: _____

Hours Per Week: _____

Dates of Activity: _____ to _____

Supervisor's Name & Title: _____

E-mail: _____

Duties: _____

_____

_____

_____

Skills Utilized: _____

_____

_____

_____

_____

Accomplishments/Honors/Awards: _____

_____

_____

Other Important Information: _____

_____

_____

High School Data Input Sheet

School Name: _____

Address: _____

_____

_____

Phone: _____

Years Attended: _____ to _____

Major Studies: _____

_____

_____

GPA/Class Rank: _____

Honors: _____

_____

_____

_____

Important Courses: _____

_____

_____

_____

Other School Data Input Sheet

School Name: _____

Address: _____

_____

_____

Phone: _____

Years Attended:_____to _____

Major Studies: _____

_____

_____

GPA/Class Rank: _____

Honors: _____

_____

_____

_____

Important Courses: _____

_____

_____

_____

College Data Input Sheet

School Name: _____

Address: _____

_____

_____

Phone: _____

Years Attended: _____ to _____

Degrees Earned: _____

Major/Minor: _____

_____

GPA/Class Rank: _____

Honors: _____

_____

_____

_____

Important Courses: _____

_____

_____

_____

Graduate School Data Input Sheet

School Name: _____

Address: _____

_____

_____

Phone: _____

Years Attended: _____ to _____

Degrees Earned: _____

Major/Minor: _____

_____

GPA/Class Rank: _____

Honors: _____

_____

_____

_____

Important Courses: _____

_____

_____

_____

Activities Data Input Sheet

Club/Activity: _____

Office(s) Held: _____

Description of Participation: _____

_____

_____

Duties/Responsibilities: _____

_____

_____

Club/Activity: _____

Office(s) Held: _____

Description of Participation: _____

_____

_____

Duties/Responsibilities: _____

_____

Club/Activity: _____

Office(s) Held: _____

Description of Participation: _____

_____

_____

Duties/Responsibilities: _____

_____

_____

Awards & Honors Data Input Sheet

Name of Award, Citation, etc.: _____

From Whom Received: _____

Date: _____

Significance: _____

_____

Other Pertinent Information: _____

_____

_____

Name of Award, Citation, etc.: _____

From Whom Received: _____

Date: _____

Significance: _____

_____

Other Pertinent Information: _____

_____

_____

Name of Award, Citation, etc.: _____

From Whom Received: _____

Date: _____

Significance: _____

_____

Other Pertinent Information: _____

_____

_____

Military Service Data Input Sheet

Branch: _____

Rank (at Discharge): _____

Dates of Service: _____ to _____

Duties & Responsibilities: _____

_____

_____

_____

Special Training and/or School Attended: _____

_____

_____

_____

Citations, Awards, etc.: _____

_____

_____

Specific Accomplishments: _____

_____

_____

_____

_____

Language Data Input Sheet

Language: _____

❑   Read   ❑   Write   ❑   Converse

Background (number of years studied, travel, etc.): __

_____

_____

_____

Language: _____

❑   Read   ❑   Write   ❑   Converse

Background (number of years studied, travel, etc.): __

_____

_____

_____

Language: _____

❑   Read   ❑   Write   ❑   Converse

Background (number of years studied, travel, etc.): __

_____

_____

_____

Chapter 2

How to Get the Information You Need

For most people, preparing for a first job interview is an exercise in self-absorption.

They spend days polishing their resumes and hours selecting the right outfits. They practice, practice, practice—to be sure they'll be ready to talk for hours about themselves and the traits that will make them terrific employees.

What's wrong with being prepared, you ask? Not a thing. But if that's all you focus on before showing up for your first interview, you will still arrive *unprepared*. You will have left out perhaps the most important step of all.

The best preparation for any job interview involves looking beyond the mirror. You must take the time to learn about the company for which you hope to work, the job for which you are interviewing and, if possible, the interviewer you will be meeting.

How can you decide if you want to work for a company until you've adequately researched it? Failure to do so could mean that within weeks of sliding behind your new desk, you'll be wondering why you ever agreed to work there in the first place!

Getting critical information about prospective employers is often not particularly difficult, although it might well be time-consuming. But such detailed company research is probably the key step most first-time interviewers skip.

What kind of salesperson are you?

To understand the importance of pre-interview preparation, think of yourself as a salesperson. Would you call on a potential customer without knowing anything about his business? If you did, how would you go about convincing him that he needed your product? Would selling him thousands of dollars of your product without knowing how well his company was doing—whether it was even financially sound—make sense?

Of course not. Then why do so many candidates show up for job interviews with only the vaguest knowledge about the company, even though they are there to sell their most important product—themselves?

Virtually every interviewer will ask a candidate what questions she has about the company. This is not merely the interviewer's way of being polite. It is a very effective technique to gauge *your* interest in the company—an important component of whether *the company* should be interested in you.

What information should you be seeking? Here is an initial list of specific questions for which you should be seeking equally specific answers:

- What are the company's leading products? What products is it looking to introduce in the near future?

- What are the company's key markets? How strong are they? What is its share of these markets?

- What are the prospects for growth and expansion? Does the company plan to grow internally or through mergers and acquisitions?

- What rate of growth does the company project over the next few years?

- To what does the company attribute fluctuations in sales?

- Has the company "downsized" or reorganized recently? What were the extent of layoffs and early retirements? Do reductions of staff seem likely in the near future?

Starting your detective work

For a very broad overview of any industry, consult the U.S. Bureau of Labor Statistics (http://stats.bls.gov), which uses business and economic trends and changing demographics to chart expected growth in employment for occupations in every industry over a 10-year period. The most current set of projections (issued in November, 1999) covers the 1998-2008 period. (Online quarterly updates of the *Occupational Outlook Handbook* are available at the same site, along with a wealth of industry and overall economic information. The most current [2000-2001] edition of *The Career Guide to Industries*, companion to the *OOH*, discusses 42 industries.)

In addition, here's a core list of research sources, most of which should be available in your local or college library:

- The *Encyclopedia of Business Information Sources* lists some 25,000 sources on more than a thousand specific subjects, including directories, associations, and more. The biannual *Directories in Print* organizes companies by industry. The annual *Job Seekers Guide to Public and Private Companies* covers 25,000 companies, with detailed information on specific job titles and openings for each. (All from Gale Research, Inc.)

- *Directory of Corporate Affiliations* and *Directory of Leading Private Companies* (Reed Reference Publishing, New Providence, NJ 07974).

- Dun and Bradstreet's family of corporate reference resources: the *Million Dollar Directory* (160,000 companies with a net worth of more than $500,000), *Top 50,000 Companies* (those with a minimum net worth of just under $2 million), and *Business Rankings* (details on the nation's top 7,500 firms). Another volume—*Reference Book of Corporate Managements/ America's Corporate Leaders*—provides detailed biographical data on the principal officers and directors of some 12,000 corporations. (Who says you can't find out about the quirks and hobbies of your interviewer?) All of these volumes are available in most libraries or from Dun's Marketing Services (3 Sylvan Way, Parsippany, NJ 07054).

- *Moody's Industry Review* (available from Moody's Investors Service, Inc., 99 Church St., New York, NY 10007).

- *Standard and Poors' Register of Corporations, Directors and Executives* includes corporate listings for more than 45,000 firms and 72,000 biographical listings (available from Standard and Poors, 25 Broadway, New York, NY 10004).

- *Thomas's Register of American Manufacturers* (Thomas Publishing Company, 1 Penn Plaza, New York, NY 10110). Annual profile of more than 150,000 manufacturers. Features information on primary products and services plus more than 100,000 trade and brand names.

- *Ward's Business Directory*, a four-volume reference work that includes listings of nearly 100,000 companies, the majority of them privately held, and details that are usually most difficult to acquire about such firms, such as number of employees, annual sales, etc. (Gale Research Inc.).

- The *Standard Directory of Advertisers* (also known as the Advertiser Red Book, because of its bright red cover) lists more than 17,000 companies that commit some portion of their budgets to advertising and promotion. It is available in two editions—classified and geographical. Major product lines and the agencies to whom they are assigned are listed, as well as names and job functions of key marketing personnel at the listed companies and their agencies.

- *The Fortune 500* is an annual compilation by *Fortune* magazine of the top U.S. businesses, ranked by sales. It will become particularly important later in your search, when you're targeting specific companies. At that time, it will enable you to analyze not only where a particular company ranks in the overall U.S. economy, but also whether it is falling or on the rise, and how it measures up against other companies in its field.

Some other potential sources of leads include *The Oxbridge Directory of Newsletters* (check your library), a listing of thousands of newsletters in a plethora of industries that might well give you some ideas and names. *The Professional Exhibits Directory* (Gale Research, Inc.) lists more than 2,000 trade shows and conventions. Why not consider attending some to learn more about the companies and products out there?

Finally, there are the major magazines you should turn to now and then to complete your research: *The Wall Street Journal*, *Barron's*, *Business Week*, *Fortune*, *Forbes*, *Industry Week*, *Nation's Business*, *National Business Employment Weekly*, and *Inc.*

Researching smaller companies

A majority of new jobs are created by small companies, but you may not learn much about them in the standard reference resources listed above. If your initial research proves fruitless or only marginally productive, try the following outside sources of information:

- The **chamber of commerce** in the community that's home to the company or division. You can find out how the company has been performing.

Has it been growing or shrinking? How many people does it employ? How many did it employ in the community two years ago? Do people consider it a good place to work?

◆ **Business/industry associations:** Many trade associations are excellent resources for industry data and statistics as well as general employment trends and specific opportunities. Four good resources are the *Encyclopedia of Associations and Business Organizations, Agencies and Publications Directory* (both from Gale Research, Inc.), *National Trade and Professional Associations of the United States* (Columbia Books, Inc.), and the *Association Yellow Pages* (Monitor Publishing Co.).

◆ **Executive, professional, and technical placement agencies:** If you are getting the job interview through an agency, see how much you can learn about the prospective employer from them.

◆ **Business editors:** Turn the tables on the news media: Ask *them* the questions! A community newspaper's business reporter or editor will usually be the person most knowledgeable about local companies. They'll know about developments at particular companies, how employees like working for them, and their reputation in the community.

◆ **Trade magazines:** Every industry has at least one trade magazine covering its developments. Call a junior (assistant or associate) editor. Ask if the publication has covered the company and if you can obtain copies of the article(s).

- ◆ **School alumni:** The college placement office, your fraternity/sorority, or alumni association might be able to tell you about someone working at the company. Alumni are usually happy to help someone from their alma mater.

- ◆ **Stockbrokers/analysts:** If the company is public, it will have an investor relations representative who can tell you which brokers and analysts "follow the stock." This means that a representative of the brokerage firm has visited with the company, written a detailed report for investors, and analyzed its industry, balance sheet, and management. Call the broker and ask for a copy of the report. It will be objective, very revealing, and give you terrific material with which to impress the interviewer.

- ◆ **Online:** There are a multitude of bulletin boards, databases, and discussion groups through which you can track down obscure information to impress a prospective employer in an interview. Your first step, of course, should be to check out the company's Web site.

Profiting from inside information

Once you've culled the *outside*—and probably more objective—sources of information, take a look at what the company tells the public about itself. After you have the interview lined up, call the interviewer's secretary or the company's investor relations department to obtain the following:

* **Annual reports.** Mark Twain said that there are three kinds of lies—"lies, damned lies, and statistics"—and you'll find all of them in most annual reports. Read between the lines of the annual report to learn as much as you can about the company.

  You will be able to tell how the company's sales and profits have been increasing or decreasing over the past few years, what its plans are for the years ahead, and the health of the industry in which it operates.

  In addition, an annual report should indicate how the company feels about its employees. Note whether the report features accomplishments of particular employees. Does it have photos of people at work? Or does it stick strictly to "the numbers" and highlight the self-aggrandizing musings of the chairman?

* **Employee handbooks.** Be gutsy. Ask the company to send you a copy of this valuable document. At the very least, the handbook will tell you about benefits, vacation time, salary review policies, and other information you might not want to ask about in the interview. It also should give you valuable insights into the company's attitude toward its employees. Is in-house training provided? Is the company picnic a much-anticipated annual event?

* **Sales/marketing brochures.** Knowing about a company's products will help you determine

whether you'd like to work for the organization and give you material upon which to base questions.

Additional sources of job leads

The previous listings should give you a plethora of information about specific companies and even help identify potential jobs. But there are other resources that are less about research than identifying specific job openings:

- Your **college or high school placement office** should be a first stop. Employers are always in touch with them, although your high school guidance counselor may be far less help, given the dearth of jobs for high school graduates.

- **Trade, technical, and business schools**— featuring courses in everything from bartending and beauty to TV repair and truck driving—offer specialized training and job placement. Because they are so specialized, they are often regularly in touch with the major employers in their industries.

- **Job fairs:** The business section of your local paper will usually include announcements of these informal get-togethers at which company recruiters and prospective employees can interact in a trade show-style atmosphere. The *Career and Job Fair Finder* (College Placement Council, Inc.) is a general resource that should be available in your library.

- **State employment agencies:** Most state laws mandate that these offices make all job openings known to everyone. You'll find them displayed on their office bulletin boards. State civil service jobs might also be advertised in specialty publications available at your local newsstand, which will also list jobs that require competitive exams.

- **Job information centers** at your local library are a good source of openings in the immediate vicinity.

- **Veterans' organizations:** If you qualify, you can get a great deal of help and information through these centers. Contact the Veterans Administration in Washington, D.C. for a list of federally funded branches and for information on privately funded veterans groups in your area. And don't forget local American Legion and VFW chapters.

- **Online job sites** have quickly become a major source of both company information and job listings. Start with the metajob boards, which allow you to search hundreds of job sites all at once. Three of the most popular are *careerbuilder.com, employment911.com*, and *jobsearchengine.com*. Then turn to the big individual sites. According to Rebecca Smith, author of *Electronic Resumes and Online Networking, 2nd Edition* (Career Press, 2000), the top 10 job-search sites as compiled by Media Matrix are:

* *www.monster.com*
* *www.careermosaic.com* (now part of *headhunter.net*)
* *www.careerpath.com* (now part of *careerbuilder.com*)
* *www.jobsearch.org*
* *www.headhunter.net*
* *www.nationjob.com*
* *www.hotjobs.com*
* *www.nettemps.com*
* *www.dice.com*
* *www.careerbuilder.com*

She also recommends two specialized sites—*www.computerjobs.com* for high- tech jobs and *www.guru.com* for freelancers, and the following sites specifically for recent college graduates or graduate students:

* *www.recruitinglinks.com*
* *www.careerhighway.com*
* *www.jobdirect.com*
* *www.jobtrak.com* (now part of *monster.com*)
* *www.mbanetwork.com*
* *www.careerpark.com*
* *www.recruitersonline.com*
* *www.alumni-network.com*

Dealing with campus recruiters

Although on-campus recruiting has become increasingly rare these days, you may be one of the lucky ones. What do you do if your first contact with a company is through a recruiter who has come to harvest the best and brightest students from your graduating class?

When you meet with a recruiter, don't be content to just sit there and answer his questions. Make it your goal to uncover the information that will help *you* ease on down the interview road.

Ask about the company's products. What other students from your school has the company hired in the past? How have they fared? Who will make the final hiring decision for the position in which you're interested?

Ask the recruiters, if they seem interested in you, to send you the annual reports, product brochures, and other materials mentioned previously.

Finding out about the interviewer

Now comes the toughest detective work of all—finding out a little bit about the person who will be firing the questions at you. This is not very important for your meeting with the recruiter in the human resources department, but it is crucial for your meeting with the hiring manager.

Let's face it, in the initial interview, you'll have perhaps 45 minutes to convince someone that you're the best candidate for the job. It'll probably help to know which are the right buttons to push to get the interviewer to notice—and *remember*—you.

Tim, a business associate of mine, asked the human re-sources department to send him back issues of the company newsletter when he was preparing to be interviewed for an open position. He then devoured the newsletters, studying everything from the opening letter from the president to the birth and wedding announcements. This enabled him to begin questions like this: "I've read that your company has recently installed a computer-integrated manufacturing system...."

Tim also learned that the company had been increasing its sales volume substantially, which led him to ask some informed questions about the company's successes. He told me that he could sense how impressed the interviewer was that he had done so much research.

But that was just the start of Tim's use of his research. The newsletters told him that his interviewer, Mr. Marty, had been with the company for 20 years and worked his way up from a lower-level job in the distribution department.

The biography in the newsletter also indicated that Marty was an avid bird-watcher. Tim did a bit of research into bird-watching—just enough to make some intelligent comments about the pictures on Marty's walls—and framed questions that demonstrated a willingness to follow a career path similar to the one his prospective boss had.

One of your key goals of the interview is to stand out in bold relief from the other candidates for the position. Tim's efforts clearly helped him do just that.

Learn more during the interview

Solid research will also prepare you to learn everything you want about the company before the conclusion of the interview. It will help you frame questions that will turn the interview into a two-way street, a learning experience for you as well as your "inquisitors."

If you've read that the organization is family-owned, find out how this might affect your prospects for promotion. If the newsletter reported that an employee opinion poll had been taken, discreetly ask for some of the results.

Asking about some of these areas can be rather delicate. We'll talk about how to frame your questions (so they are taken as brilliant indications of your interest and not insulting examples of your insensitivity) in Chapter 9.

Chapter 3

How to Get in
the Door

Although nobody likes doing it, homework does have its payoffs. Especially during a job hunt. From the research you doggedly pursued on prospective employers, you should have learned several important things about each:

- What it's looking for in its employees.
- Its key products and markets.
- Whether it's hired employees from your school, with your degree, and how they've fared.
- Who the hiring manager is and what type of people he usually hires.
- Why you might enjoy working for that company.

All of this information will prove invaluable to you, not only during the interview, but in helping you get the interview in the first place.

Who can you turn to?

Whether you're answering a classified advertisement or launching an all-out assault on the best companies in the industry you've chosen, you'll want to write to the hiring manager, *not* the human resources department.

The reason is quite simple. Human resources departments usually have little idea about what the hiring manager really wants in a job applicant. The more technical or specialized the field, the truer this statement.

I've known of a human resources director who recommended a candidate for whom English was a second—and not very *good*—language for the top editorial post on a major association magazine. Another passed along a candidate who got 55 out of 100 on a spelling test for a proofreading position. Still another recommended someone whose resume was filled with rather obvious or easily discovered lies for a vice president of finance position.

At many organizations, hiring managers make it a point to go around their human resources departments—bringing candidates in, interviewing them, and only *then* passing them along so human resources can take care of the paperwork.

Make it easier for the hiring manager to do just that. Make every effort to get in touch with him or her yourself.

That winning letter

The letter on page 58 was written by a candidate who is about to get out of college and stride tentatively into the workaday world. Let's take a look at several of the key components of this letter:

1. It's typed on the applicant's letterhead—a nice, professional touch. Design and print your own letterhead and envelopes. Use a quality letter stock in white, off-white, or buff. (Your resume should be printed on the same stock.) The typeface used is a common, readable one, not overly busy, or ornate.

2. It addresses, by name and title, the manager with the authority to hire. (Naturally the applicant had the good sense and professionalism to triple-check the spelling of both the name and title! Even simple first and last names, like Steven/Stephen or Fry/Frye, can trip you up.)

3. The first paragraph immediately states the reason the applicant wrote the letter. It indicates the specific job or type of work for which he was applying and where (or from whom) he learned about the opening.

4. The second and third paragraphs contain his sales pitch: why he should be considered for the job, what he can offer the company, and why he deserves an interview.

5. It's lively. It refers to the resume and tells the hiring manager a little more about the candidate without overdoing it. As a college student, you don't have a plethora of experience with which to sell a prospective employer. While it's important to mention such things as internships, don't oversell them.

6. It mentions the name of the company and some fact about it. This sets the letter apart from so many of the form letters job seekers send out.

7. This letter provides absolutely no information that is not related to the job. If a manager wants to learn more, she will make an attempt to do so during the interview. But she is *not* interested in slogging through a lot of extraneous information in a letter.

8. It's important to keep the letter to one page, as did this candidate. Anything more might lead some managers to toss it...unread.

A couple of other cautions: Always type, never handwrite, the manager's name and address on the envelope. And, if you have a summer job, do not send the letter through your employer's postage meter. It makes you look like a petty crook. Spring for your own stamp.

Okay, sometimes you *should* use human resources

I have stressed the importance of writing your letter to the real decision-maker, the hiring manager. However, sometimes it *is* advisable to contact the human resources department, especially given your current lack of experience.

If you have targeted a particular company, but are not sure whether any job openings exist, get in touch with the director of human resources, again, by name. Tell him the reasons that you'd like to work for the company, the positions you think you'd be qualified for, and something about yourself and your accomplishments.

The follow-up phone call

You've sealed your message in the bottle and thrown it out to sea. The optimists among you will expect their telephones to ring off the hook with job offers within two days. Pessimists will expect to hear nothing.

Unfortunately, in most cases, the pessimists will be right. When your letter produces nothing, you will probably feel depressed. You just won't believe that some lucky company out there has been given the chance to hire you and hasn't jumped at it. It's probably unrealistic of you to feel quite so surprised. After all, that company you're interested in working for *has* been thriving without you for some time.

What do you do? Well, to borrow a phrase from sales-motivation speakers, "Make it happen!" And the way to make it happen, as every salesperson knows, is to follow up your letter with a phone call.

I suggest waiting about a week after you've posted your letter to call. However, I advise against calling on Monday or Friday, first thing in the morning, toward 5 p.m., or during the lunch shift. In other words, place your call between 10 a.m. and noon, or between 2:30 p.m. and 4 p.m. on Tuesday, Wednesday, or Thursday.

If you've cited a network connection in your letter to a prospective employer or if your skills are a match for an opening at their company, you'll probably hear back from someone. If you don't hear back within a week or so, or by the time the secretary told you that someone might call, call again. Remember, *always* be pleasant on the phone. A secretary or assistant who takes a disliking to you can torpedo your hopes of landing a job.

"Don't call us..."

If you call a second time and still get *nada*, you'll know that you're in "don't-call-us-we'll-call-you" hell. It's probably best to give up (unless you have another connection that you can follow up).

If you receive a letter acknowledging receipt of your resume, but rejecting your application, follow up with a note thanking the person for responding and asking her to keep you in mind for any future openings.

The letter should read something like the one on page 59—it shows that you are attentive, courteous, and somewhat aggressive.

What if they *do* call you?

If, on the other hand, someone calls you with a positive response to your letter, stay calm—and don't drop the phone!

In fact, you should be at least somewhat prepared for this to happen. An increasing number of companies are prescreening candidates on the telephone to save time and reduce recruitment costs.

The hiring manager or a representative from the human resources department will have a battery of questions for you. We will discuss the content of these questions in Chapter 5. Relax. You'll be ready.

If you do secure the interview, follow up with a confirming note. It should be something like the letter on page 60.

Well, the easy part is over. You've secured your chance to interview for a job. You've done your homework on the company. You've written the best letter of your life. And you've sold yourself in writing and over the telephone.

But that's only the beginning. Now you must prepare and rehearse for your interview and endure the emotional seesaw between hope and dread. However, the following chapters can help assure that that emotional seesaw ends up being a joyride.

RESPONDING TO AN AD

Gregory L. Wright
104 Highland Avenue
Yorktown Heights, NY 11345
914-555-1237
E-mail: LazelleW@college.com

February 24, 2002

Mr. Robert Carr, Vice President, Sales
ABC Sportswear
1315 Broadway
New York, NY 10036

Dear Mr. Carr:

   The sales trainee position at ABC Sportswear briefly described in your February 23 advertisement in *The New York Times* is very appealing to me. Please accept this letter and the attached resume as application for this opening.

   While majoring in business (with a marketing minor) at Wallace State, I worked on a number of special projects that helped me develop some of the skills mentioned in your ad. Specifically, I gained a great deal of knowledge about budgeting, telemarketing, and account analysis.

   As a summer intern for Reebok, I was able to refine some of my skills as I worked with the promotion department to develop a sales-call management system. My internship at Shaw Electronics gave me experience in helping establish a database marketing program.

   I would like to meet with you at your convenience to discuss this position and my qualifications for it in more detail. I learned a great deal about ABC from your campus recruiter, Nick Deane, and think it would be a terrific place to work.

   Thank you for your time. I look forward to meeting with you.

Sincerely yours,

Gregory Wright

RESPONDING TO REJECTION

Eugene Rutigliano
7 Lobell Court, West Orange, NJ 07009
201-748-2098
E-mail: Huge@rutigliano.net

July 10, 2002

Mr. David Basting
Director of Public Relations
Wonder Drug, Inc.
One Wonder Plaza
Harmon Meadow, NJ 07123

Dear Mr. Basting:

Naturally, I was disappointed that there are no positions open for me at this time at Wonder Drug, Inc. As I indicated in my letter of July 1, I have long been an admirer of your company and thought that my skills in marketing would make me a valuable contributor.

I am enclosing another copy of my resume that I hope you will keep on file in the event that a position for which you think I am qualified becomes available.

I look forward to hearing from you some time in the future.

Sincerely yours,

Eugene Rutigliano

CONFIRMING AN INTERVIEW

Eugene Rutigliano
7 Lobell Court, West Orange, NJ 07009
201-748-2098
E-mail: Huge@rutigliano.net

July 10, 2002

Mr. David Basting
Director of Public Relations
Wonder Drug, Inc.
One Wonder Plaza
Harmon Meadow, NJ 07123

Dear Mr. Basting:
  I am looking forward to meeting with you on August 15 at 9:30 a.m. to discuss the opening in your department. I am very excited about the chance to work for your company as assistant director of solid waste management.
  Thank you for the opportunity.

Sincerely yours,

Eugene Rutigliano

Chapter 4

How to Create
Your Network

Career experts estimate that as many as 80 percent of all available jobs are *never advertised*! That can put you at a real disadvantage in a highly competitive job market. If you don't have access to the opportunities, you surely won't get the interviews.

How can you increase your chances to get the job you really want? By building on a resource you already have close at hand—your network. You don't have a network, you say? Trust me. *Everyone* has a network—family, friends, professors, past and present co-workers (you get the picture). These people also know a lot of other people (through *their* networks). In fact, they may know someone who holds the job you're interested in or, better yet, who works in the company you're targeting.

Would your uncle mind if you called or wrote a letter to his golf buddy who just happens to be marketing manager at XYZ

Company? Chances are, he'll pave the way with a phone call. All of a sudden, you have an "in."

That is how most people get jobs—through informal, personal connections.

The means *is* the end

At the outset of your career, it's tempting to think of networking as a means to an end—getting your first job. But I encourage you to look farther ahead. You don't need me to remind you that these are turbulent times. Given the "last hired, first fired" philosophy of some firms, you may be "downsized" before you've had a chance to check out the executive washroom. What will you do then?

If you've kept in touch with all the people you added to your network this time around, your task will be that much easier the next time. Yes, that means building and maintaining a mutually beneficial relationship with each of your connections.

Sounds exhausting, doesn't it? But it doesn't have to be. Rather than getting together every week, you may check in by phone once or twice a year, send off a note with an article that might be of interest to a former colleague, or refer someone who, earlier, made an introduction for you.

The fact is, you can never know what twists and turns your career will take or what kind of information you'll need down the road. Your fate often rests on the extent and, later, the quality of your connections.

A web of relationships

While the term "networking" didn't gain prominence until the 1970s, it is by no means a new phenomenon. Networking is the process of turning to relatives, friends, and acquaintances to secure the information—and possibly even referrals—that will help you find a job. Networking will help you identify where jobs are and give you the background and personal introductions necessary to pursue them.

Most importantly, networking works, because it's based on a decidedly human prejudice—the desire to "fit in" with a group. In a way, it's a built-in screening process.

Six good reasons to network

Some people are loathe to participate in the networking process because they don't want to "bother" other people with their own selfish demands. Nonsense! There are at least half a dozen excellent reasons most people will be *happy* to help you:

1. **Someday you'll return the favor.** An ace insurance salesman built a successful business by offering low-cost coverage to first-year medical students. Ten years later, these now-successful practitioners remembered the company (and the salesman) that helped them when they were just getting started. He gets new referrals every day.

2. **They need you just as much as you need them.** If you sense that your "brain is being picked" about the latest techniques of computer graphics, be forthcoming with your information. Schools and universities are often at the forefront of technology, so why not let the interviewer

"audit" your course? It may be the reason she agreed to see you in the first place.

3. **You make them look important.** Internal politics can be a powerful motivator. Some people will see you to make themselves appear powerful, implying to others that they have the authority to hire.

4. **They know it's better to be safe than sorry.** Nobody knows better than today's hiring managers how quickly things can change. Someone may give notice tomorrow. A new client may stretch staff resources to the limits. By maintaining a backlog of qualified candidates, they can move quickly to hire the best people.

5. **They've been in your shoes.** Some people will see you because they know how you feel. They've been there, and they feel that "giving back" is the decent thing to do.

6. **They want to keep their own "net" working.** Most people are anxious to do a friend (whoever referred you) a favor. If a colleague is seeking new talent, you might represent a referral. You see, networking never really stops—it helps them, and it helps you.

Creating the ideal network

Here's how to identify and enrich your current network:

1. **Diversify.** You never know who might be in a position to help, so don't limit your contacts to just relatives and close friends. The wider you cast your net, the more (and more kinds of) fish you'll catch.

2. **Include everybody.** Your initial networking list should include just about every living, breathing person you know. That includes your friends, relatives, social acquaintances, classmates, college alumni, professors, teachers, dentist, doctor, family lawyer, insurance agent, banker, travel agent, elected officials in your community, clergy, members of your religious group, local tradespeople, local business owners, and social club officers. Ultimately, you'll include everybody *they* know!

3. **Make specific requests.** Calling everyone and simply asking for "whatever help you can give me" is unfair to the people you're calling—and not very effective. Instead, make a list of the kinds of assistance you'll need from the people in your network. Then make specific requests of each person. Do they know of jobs at their company? Can they introduce you to the proper executives? Have they heard something about or do they know someone at the company you're planning to interview with next week? The more organized you are, the easier it will be to figure out who might have the information you need.

4. **Value your contacts.** Keep those who have provided helpful information or introductions informed about how your job search turns out. Such courtesy will be appreciated and may lead to more contacts. If someone you call has nothing to offer today, make a note to yourself to call her back in a few months.

5. **Maintain good records.** Keep your contact list up-to-date. Detailed records—with whom you

spoke, when, about what, etc.—will help you keep
track of your overall progress and organize what
can quickly become an unwieldy process.

Interviewing for information

There's a great difference between a job interview (what
you're eventually after) and an informational interview (which
I'm going to prepare you for right now).

This technique works because there is no pressure on
the interviewer (your new contact) to give you a job. In an
informational interview, information is the only thing you're
after—information that you hope will someday *get* you a job,
just not necessarily *today*.

In an informational interview, your goal is to learn as much
as you can about the industry, company, and job you've targeted. A meeting with someone already doing what you soon
hope to be doing is by far the best way to find out everything
you need to know before you walk through the door and sit
down for a formal job interview. Don't be shy about this. You'll
find that most people are happy to talk about their jobs.

If you learn of a specific job opening during an informational interview, you are in a position to find out many important
details about it. You may also find out who will be doing the
interviewing and, if you're lucky, gain some valuable insight
into his experience and personality. With your contact's permission, you may also be able to use her name as a referral.

What it's all about

There are, ideally, six specific goals you hope to fulfill during each informational interview:

1. To unearth current information about the industry, company, and pertinent job functions.

2. To investigate each company's hiring policies, especially to identify key decision-makers.

3. To sell yourself and leave a calling card—your resume.

4. To get advice that will help you define and refine your job search.

5. To obtain referrals to people who can give you even more information.

6. To develop a list of follow-up activities in order to heighten your visibility among key contacts.

"But who has time to meet with me?"

As the head of a publishing company, I get quite a few requests for such informational interviews every year. I always agree to see candidates who send well-written letters and indicate that they clearly understand that my company has no job openings (even if I know we do).

I have several reasons for making time in a very busy schedule for such job seekers:

- ◆ My company keeps a file of promising candidates that we use when we want to add staff.

- ◆ I have colleagues and recruiters in *my* network to whom I want to refer good candidates.

- ◆ I like to know how my company is perceived by job seekers.

- ◆ I want to help recent college graduates facing the same obstacles I faced way back when.

I am happy to provide an overview of the publishing market, information on starting salaries for the types of jobs these individuals are seeking, and, if I am impressed by them, to refer them to colleagues.

Candidates leave my office (hopefully) armed with valuable information that will come in handy in future interviews and, if the interview went well, with more confidence.

Setting up an informational interview

Where do you begin? Preferably in a quiet room with a piece of paper on which you will write:

1. The names of everyone you know who might be in a position to hire you.
2. The names of everyone you know who might know someone who might be in a position to hire you.

These lists will *not* be short if you remember to include the names of your friends, relatives, social acquaintances, classmates, college alumni, professors, teachers, dentist, doctor, family lawyer, insurance agent, banker, travel agent, elected officials in your community, clergy, members of your religious group, local tradepersons, local business owners, social club officers…and anyone else you can think of!

Then, begin calling or visiting each of these people. If you don't know someone particularly well, introduce yourself by making a *specific request*. Tell your network connection what you've studied in school, the type of job you're interested in landing, and the companies you'd like to join. Ask if she knows someone already working in your chosen career. If, for example, your professor gives you the names and telephone numbers of some of his former students, be sure to ask if you can use his name when you call or write them. Your letters should read something like the one on page 75.

I know that you might have to overcome some shyness and embarrassment to call people and ask for help. But you'll be surprised at how delighted people are that *you thought they could help you.*

The follow-through

Your follow-up phone calls requesting informational interviews will be similar to those we discussed in the last chapter. You'll probably be stonewalled by an executive secretary, but you should be polite and persistent.

Remember to refer to the date and subject of the letter and say, "I wrote to [Mr. or Ms. X] at the suggestion of..." This will help increase the chances that your message will go to the top of the pile.

If you are successful in landing an informational interview, send a confirming letter restating the date, time, and reason for the appointment.

The informational interview

When the awaited day finally arrives for you to meet with your contact, dress in your best business attire (see Chapter 6 for more on this) and arrive a few minutes early, so that you have adequate time to freshen up. Then take a deep breath and try to relax in the reception area before you are called. It will help to remember two things:

1. This is *not* a job interview. This takes the pressure off both you and your contact. This meeting is simply an opportunity for you to gather information and, possibly, a reference. During the interview, of course, you will become *known* to your contact, so that when a new opportunity does arise, you may be just the person that comes to mind.

2. *You* are in charge of the interview. You are the one who will be posing most of the questions.

When you finally get to meet your contact, greet her warmly and express your gratitude for this opportunity. Your meeting should go something like this:

You: *Thanks for taking time out of your busy scheule to meet with me, Ms. Burns. I've heard and read a lot about you.*

Contact: *Not at all. Jay and I go way back and he told me that you were really going places. I hope I can help. I think my secretary told you we have a hiring freeze on right now.*

Y: *Yes. I've read about how hard the hotel industry has been hit by the recession and the events of 9-11. But things seem to be turning around now. Am I right?*

C: *Yes, but slowly. The building boom has stopped, of course. And while business people are starting to travel again, we're just beginning to see signs that vacation travel is picking up again. Our company came through this okay. We're beginning to experience a turnaround.*

Y: *Ms. Burns, I wanted to see you to ask you some questions that will help me get started in the hotel business. I've always wanted to work in the travel field and my studies at Howard Johnson's have convinced me that sales and marketing is the area I want to be in. Where's the best place for me to get my start?*

C: *Well, you'll have to start in sales or public relations. Hotels are fairly unsophisticated about marketing. People with marketing in their title often started out in the sales department of a single hotel. That's how I got my start.*

Y: *Should I apply to chain headquarters or to the individual properties to land an entry-level sales job?*

C: *Both. However, most of the junior sales positions are filled at the property level. If I were you, I'd try some of the larger convention properties that have large sales forces, like the Holiday Regency downtown here.*

Y: *Should I expect to be doing telephone sales for a while?*

C: *Yes. Then, if you perform well, you'll be given a "territory," such as religious conventions or travel agents, to call on.*

Y: *What entry-level salary should I expect?*

C: *Somewhere in the low 20s. We're starting people off at $23,000 when we have the rare position to fill.*

> **Y:**   *Are there more jobs in some areas of the country than others?*
>
> **C:**   *Right now, it's the Northeast that's suffering. Everyone wants to be in the Sun Belt and resort destinations. Las Vegas is one city where the hotel business is always healthy.*
>
> **Y:**   *I've also thought about joining an advertising agency that specializes in the hotel business. Can you recommend any that you've worked with?*

The interview proceeds like this for some time. Your contact has become comfortable, having by now realized that you're not there to harass her into hiring you. The questions have made her forget that this is, after all, a thinly disguised job interview. She gives you a lot of solid information, the names of some advertising agencies and hotel executives to contact—and permission to use her name when you do. You diligently write these down.

In the meantime, you have made a favorable impression on her by demonstrating that you know the hotel industry and some of its key players. You also have demonstrated that you are a job candidate with well-defined career goals.

After the interview

The very day of the interview (or the next morning if you had an afternoon or early evening appointment) dash off letters of thanks both to your contact *and* to the person who referred you to her. Include a copy of your resume in the letter to your new contact, requesting that she pass it on to anyone looking for a qualified entry-level candidate. Then, start the networking process all over again with the names you acquired from the informational interview. One of these is bound to land you a *real* job interview, the subject of the next chapter.

Keep detailed, up-to-date records

Get the results of each interview down on paper and create a file called your "Interview Recap Record." Record the following information on an index card, in a notebook or, ideally, in a computer database. It should be set up something like this:

Name: XYZ Company

Address: 22 Sheridan Place, Elmira, NY 14902

Phone: (607) 555-8291

Contact: Dennis L. Bartlett

Type of Business: Aircraft Engine Manufacturer

Referral Contact: Michael Swantic, Fidelity National Bank

Date: September 23, 2001

Results: Add a one- or two-paragraph summary of what you found out at the meeting. State the facts (what you found out in response to your specific questions) as well as your *impressions* (your assessment of the opportunities for further discussions, your "gut feeling" about your chances of being considered for future openings). Based on your interview with XYZ Corp., you might include the following:

XYZ looks to college-trained personnel to fill its entry-level finance slots. Operations are centralized. Company emphasizes full employee understanding of all facets of operations and encourages interdepartmental transfers. Work environment is low-key. Finance is seen as a growth area based on the company's prior hiring record and the growing importance of global trade. Mr. Bartlett seemed impressed with my resume and general presentation. I could tell from the pictures on his office wall that he is an outdoors type. (He also plays tennis!)

Ann Marie Sharp
1333 Stanton Avenue
Lubbock, TX 45678
Phone: 222-555-4444
E-mail: AMS@lol.reg

April 30, 2002

Ms. Karen Burns
Vice President of Marketing
The Crimson Hotel Group
3333 LBJ Parkway
Houston, TX 46810

Dear Ms. Burns:

I am writing at the suggestion of Jay Bernstein at ABC Travel. He knows of my interest in the hotel field and, given your experience at The Crimson Hotel Group, thought you might be able to help me learn more about the industry and how I might get my career off to a flying start.

As I finish up my studies at the Howard Johnson Hotel and Restaurant School at Orange County State, I am doing everything I can to gain a better understanding of the "real world" of hotel sales and marketing, my particular field of study.

If you could spare a few minutes to meet with me during the week of May 13, when I will be visiting the Houston area, I'm certain you could give me the direction I need.

I will call your office next week to see if we can schedule an appointment. I look forward to meeting you.

Sincerely,

Ann Marie Sharp
cc: Jay Bernstein

Chapter 5

What to Expect During Your First Interview

For employers, interviewing has made the transition from art to science. Like scientists, interviewers are now expected to gather detailed information on all the specimens they study: information that can be measured, quantified, and accurately compared. In fact, sometimes it seems as if quantification has replaced qualification in the hiring process.

Employers want to know a lot more than even the most detailed job application could ever tell them. So they're testing more—your honesty, intelligence, mental health, even the toxicity of your blood are all fair game. And they're interviewing more candidates, whom they're putting through *more* interviews with *more* interviewers.

The screening interview

If you are going for a job at a mid-sized or large company (any organization of more than about 250 employees), your first interview will often be with an employment or staffing manager in the human resources department. More and more often, this interview is taking candidates by surprise. Why? Because many companies have begun conducting the initial screening interview by phone in an effort to save time and/or do more with less staff.

You may also be screened via telephone by a hiring manager or executive at a small company, some of whom rely on telephone screening as a primary means of taking the measure of job candidates. For them, the in-person interview is often little more than an opportunity to confirm what they believe they have already learned about you.

Therefore, because this will probably not be scheduled in advance, you must begin preparing for the telephone interview as soon as you send out your resumes and letters.

Handling the telephone screener

The scene could go something like this: You're sitting at home having your orange juice on a warm summer day three weeks after graduation. The phone rings. You saunter over to answer it, casting sidelong glances at the headlines on the morning newspaper and scratching your stomach.

"Hello," you groan.

"Good morning," says the almost too chipper voice on the other end. "This is Molly Ackroyd of ABC Widget. I'm looking for Joseph Lerman."

"Speaking."

"Oh, hello. May I call you Joe? You applied for our opening in the solid waste management department, and I'm calling to ask you some preliminary questions."

You're about to freeze. You gulp, almost audibly. Your head swims from a rush of adrenaline. You begin looking for a way out. You consider saying, "O-O-Oh, you want Joseph *Lerman*. I'm afraid he's not here right now. Can I take a message?"

But you think better of it. Let's take a look at who Molly is and why she's calling you.

Just the facts

Molly is a lower-level person in the HR department who has been trained in some fairly basic interview techniques. Odds are that she hasn't been out of college much longer than you, and she has only a bare-bones idea of the duties and responsibilities of the position for which you've applied.

Her job has a rather simple goal: to reduce the number of bona fide candidates before any of them get a chance to even walk in the door.

After you've gotten through the preliminaries with Molly, her end of the conversation will follow a script. She will be asking questions to see if you have the easily quantifiable qualifications for the position—the right degree, command of the English language, the right types of internships or other experience, willingness to relocate, whatever.

Primarily, Molly will be trying to determine if you've been truthful on your resume.

The interview will also be somewhat qualitative: How well have you responded to her surprise phone call? And how quickly did you recover from the shock? Do you exhibit sufficient enthusiasm for the position? Do you exhibit any obvious emotional disturbances? How articulate are you? How energetic? How prepared? Should she or anybody else at Widget go out on a limb and actually recommend you for a job?

Because you are new to the job-hunting process, some nervousness at a time like this is perfectly normal. So take a deep breath and slowly exhale before you say anything.

"Oh, Ms. Ackroyd, I'm so glad you called. What can I do for you this morning?"

Now, smile. Although Molly can't see you, your smile will automatically make your voice sound more enthusiastic—this is a trick taught to all telephone salespeople and customer-service employees. In addition, form a mental picture of Molly. Conjure up someone pleasant and nonthreatening, and imagine that she's the person you're talking to. And don't forget to breathe between sentences.

Your first response already has shown enthusiasm and a willingness to be cooperative. Because Molly might have 25 of these calls to make today, she'll be very grateful to you for making her job easier and more pleasant.

Remember, the telephone interview is a screening-*out,* not a screening-in process. Molly is trying to reduce the number of in-person interviews she, her supervisor, and the hiring manager must conduct.

In other words, Molly desperately wants to scratch 24 of the 25 candidates she calls today off her list. The following tips can help you beat these odds:

- **Make it easy** for Molly to reach you—buy an answering machine if there is any time during business hours that your phone might not be answered.

- **Be cheerful and enthusiastic.** Remember to smile while you're speaking on the phone.

- ◆ **Be prepared.** Keep handy a copy of your resume and cover letter and some basic facts about ABC Widget and the other companies to which you've applied.

- ◆ **Stay in control.** If you don't have documents near the phone, if you're in your underwear and the doorbell has just rung, ask Molly to hold on a few seconds or offer to call her right back. Do it calmly and don't think you'll put her off. She knows she's caught you by surprise.

- ◆ **Buy yourself some time** to think by rephrasing Molly's questions and repeating them back to her. (Just don't repeat them verbatim. You'll sound as annoying as a parrot.) For example:

  Molly: *"Please tell me a little bit about your internship at XYZ Dump."*

  You: *"Ah, my internship last summer at XYZ? That was a terrific experience for me. I learned a great deal about solid waste management. For instance..."*

This is a means of "warming up" for your reply, or remembering those answers I hope you have rehearsed before now. It is also another way for you to calm yourself down and keep that natural anxiety from turning the interview into a natural disaster.

- ◆ **Make sure to ask** for the correct spelling of Molly's name, her complete title, and the address of the company office she works in. You'll want to follow up the telephone interview with a letter thanking her for calling and reaffirming your interest in the position.

- ◆ **Don't volunteer anything.** The telephone interviewer is out to get facts and assess the truthfulness of your application. If you volunteer something more, you might inadvertently give her a reason to reject you. If you abruptly switched majors, entered and left graduate school, resigned from an internship or part-time job, let Molly ask before you tell. Tell the truth when she *does* ask, but don't feel the need to unburden yourself if she doesn't.

The in-person screening interview

Let's face it, the deck is stacked against you when Molly calls. She wants to speak once and only once to as many people that day as possible. It's more difficult to put your best foot forward over the telephone. And, if the company is not in a remote location, it probably is using telephone screening because so many apparently qualified candidates applied for the position. Yes, that's right. You're not the only one who's heard about that terrific job at ABC Widget.

On the other hand, the live screening interview gives you a better chance to make a good impression (we'll discuss that more in the next chapter), and probably is an indication that there's a relatively small cadre of candidates or that your application is held in at least relatively high regard.

That's the good news.

The bad news is that the live, and usually longer, interview gives Molly or one of her senior colleagues the chance to use more sophisticated interview techniques.

She'll also have a chance to pass judgment on more than your words and the sound of your voice. She'll be, as the pessimists might put it, watching you squirm.

To avoid wriggling like a worm under a microscope, you must work at getting your emotions under control *before* the in-person interview with Molly begins.

Arrive early. If your appointment is at 9 a.m., aim to arrive at the building by 8:30, so you won't get overly flustered about finding the right office or being late. If you're from out of town, consider arriving the night before for any interview—even if it means paying for an inexpensive hotel room.

Freshen up. Proceed to the reception area 15 to 20 minutes before the scheduled start of the interview. Tell the receptionist that you are there to see Ms. Ackroyd, but that you would first like to use the restroom. Take that opportunity to wash your hands and make sure that your hair and clothing are all in order. Look to see that there are no scuff marks on your shoes. Looking spiffy? Good. It's time to meet Molly.

The trained interviewer's arsenal

Let's take a look at the techniques that Molly will use once you've passed muster over the telephone. Remember, she is trained and practiced in the science of interviewing to a degree that has probably never been even dreamed of by the hiring manager—the person you're hoping to work for (unless of course you're applying for a job in the HR department). And it is the hiring manager, you know, who will really decide if you'll be walking to work or still walking the pavement next week. Nevertheless, Molly Ackroyd is the gatekeeper. So it's just as important to impress her.

The structured or database interview

The most basic of all interviews is what has come to be known as the structured or database interview. Although this might sound complicated or highly technological, both terms refer only to the fact that the interviewer must be careful to ask the same comprehensive set of questions of all candidates.

By asking exactly the same set of questions of every candidate, the theory goes, the interviewer will be able to accurately and fairly compare them. In other words, it allows the hiring organization to establish a complete database on each candidate (the term has nothing to do with computers, although computers might be used to store, retrieve, and organize the data gathered) so that eventually it's comparing "apples to apples."

The structured interview can be conducted by more than one person. You will notice interviewers in these situations referring to a long list of questions, checking off things or writing out summaries of your answers.

Because of its comprehensiveness, the structured interview will drain you. You must be prepared to answer questions about your education, related experiences, personal likes and dislikes, interpersonal skills, management skills, if you've supervised other people, and just about anything else connected to your skills, personality, experience, and "potential."

If you haven't reviewed your personal inventory sheets prior to this type of interview, you will be unable to answer a number of questions about yourself—a situation guaranteed to make you look and feel pretty stupid.

The targeted interview

The targeted interview is narrower in scope, with nearly all of the questions designed to mine information about the specific skills the employer has deemed necessary for success on the job that's available.

During a targeted interview for a sales position in a remote office, for instance, you might be asked many questions about your interpersonal skills, your self-discipline, and the degree to which you procrastinate.

The problem with this type of interview for the candidate is that only a part of the "real you" is given the chance to shine through. You might have several strengths that mitigate a weakness in one area, but the interviewer might not give you the chance to demonstrate them.

How to ace a structured or targeted interview

Keep your answers terse, but thorough. You might hope that the interviewer asks you about different parts of your background, but don't talk about areas the interviewer doesn't ask about. The interviewer wants you to give him the facts in a structured format—and only the facts that he is asking about.

Be prepared to answer many questions about just one part of your background or personality. The company has deemed this area an important one for your success.

The situational interview

"Let's suppose everyone but you called in sick and..." Questions like this will tell you that you are in the midst of the increasingly popular situational interview.

Like the targeted interview, the situational interview is geared toward measuring the degree to which candidates demonstrate traits deemed key for success in a given position.

The interviewer elicits this information by posing a series of real or hypothetical situations and asking how the candidate would act in each one.

Usually companies are trying to measure candidates' resourcefulness, logic, conceptual thinking ability, creativity, and logical thinking.

How to ace a situational interview

Situational interviews allow you to really shine if you:

- ◆ Avoid the bull. No type of interview technique invites candidates to be boastful, to exaggerate, or to downright fabricate more than the situational interview. But no other technique exposes that tendency in a candidate so effectively.

- ◆ Show that you have a grasp of the real world and that you realize you have a lot to learn about the business. This will be much more effective than trying to act like Donald Trump.

- ◆ Think through your answers. "You're faced with a production deadline and several people in your department have called in sick..." "Your biggest customer says he's tired of having the company change salesmen on him and he's taking all of his business to a competitor..." Before you glibly announce that you'd just hire temps or make reservations at the city's best restaurant, think about the possible results and repercussions of your decisions.

The team interview

The team interview can range from a pleasant conversation with a number of your potential colleagues to a torturous interrogation. Typically, you will meet with a group or team of interviewers around a conference table. They may be members of your prospective department or a cross-section of employees from throughout the company. The hiring manager or someone from human resources may chair an orderly question-and-answer session...or allow the group to shoot questions at you like a firing squad. When it's over, the entire group may vote on your candidacy.

Will majority rule? Does it have to be unanimous? Can a single person who simply didn't like your looks really torpedo your chances?

It all depends on the company. In some, the hiring manager will poll the group for their "votes" and make whatever decision he wants to anyway! In others, unanimity is not required but is certainly preferred to a "three to three" tie-break situation.

Is the team interview good for you? Well, you have to convince more people you're worthy, but you may have had to do that anyway, just one at a time. A group may well ask a broader range of questions that allow you to truly strut your stuff...or quickly uncover your flaws. Just treat every member equally— you'll rarely be able to identify with any certainty the real power at the table...or even if there is one. And be diplomatic, advice that will serve you well in any interview situation. After all, the policy you're happily criticizing today may have been proposed by the hiring manager yesterday!

The stress interview

Formal qualifications are important, but in some jobs, the emotional demands, sudden emergencies, and breakneck pace of work can be downright intimidating—not once in a while, but every day. Even a candidate who knows all the technical moves may wilt under the glare of an etiquette-challenged boss or crumble when inheriting a surrealistically compressed deadline.

When you're interviewing for such a position—whether you're seeking a job as a stockbroker, an air traffic controller, or a prison guard—an interviewer may feel it's not enough to ascertain that you are capable of performing the job under the *best* conditions. He may well try to find out for sure how you will do under the very *worst* conditions. And that's where the stress interview comes in.

Anyone who's been through one of these never forgets it. The stress interview is designed to cut through the veneer of pleasantries to the heart of the matter and see what a candidate is really made of. A common enough question in this setting could sound gruff or rude, which is exactly how it's *supposed* to sound.

How to ace a stress interview

- **Never let them see you sweat.** In other words, no matter how stressful the situation, stay calm. Never take your eyes from the interviewer. When she finishes asking a question, take a few seconds to compose yourself and then, and only then, answer.

- **Recognize the situation for what it is**—nothing more than an artificial scenario designed to see how you react under pressure. The interviewer probably has nothing against you personally.

- **Don't become despondent.** It's easy to think that the interviewer has taken a strong dislike to you and that your chances for completing the interview process are nil. That's not the case. The stress interview is designed to see if you will become depressed, hostile, and flustered when the going gets tough.

◆ **Watch your tone of voice.** It's easy to become sarcastic during a stress interview, especially if you don't realize what the interviewer is up to.

Lastly, you may question seeking a job with a company that utilizes such techniques. If they think insulting and belittling you during the interview are effective tools, what's their management philosophy—bread, water, and torture?

Why you're a puzzle to HR

It is not the purpose of this book to frighten you. But forewarned, as they say, is forearmed.

As someone with little or no experience, you represent something of a conundrum for human resource professionals. They are well-schooled in interview theory, and the belief that holds sway in the field is that "past performance and behavior are the single most reliable factors known in predicting future performance and behavior" (according to Richard H. Beatty, president of the Bradford Group, an executive search firm).

Given the fact that you have no experience, you don't fit in with the basic theory of interviews. Zealous screening interviewers, therefore, will be trying to ferret out information about your college performance, your personality, and your personal, interactive style that will be predictive of "future performance."

As a new kid on the block, you are making their job a little more difficult to do well, or to do as scientifically. They might not like that, and might be more tempted to try out hypothetical questions, stress techniques, and other means to get at the real you.

A track record would obviate the need for this type of performance test.

This might seem awfully complicated. But remember, human resources professionals are usually the only people at a company trained in sophisticated interviewing techniques. However, the interview with the hiring manager, as we'll see in Chapter 7, has its own challenges and opportunities for you to demonstrate why you're the best person for the job.

Chapter 6

Make the Right First Impression

You don't get a second chance to make a first impression.

If there's one notion that all interviewers share, it's that you, as a candidate, are giving them your very best shot. They are convinced that what they see and hear during the interview—the way you're dressed, the degree of politeness you exhibit, your demeanor, your social skills—are the best you've got.

After all, you're trying to convince a total stranger that he should invest substantial amounts of time and money in you. Why wouldn't you look and act your best?

Now, I'm sure some of you think you look best in a tank top and cutoffs, and you might be right, but a job interview is one time in your life when it's probably best to keep your wardrobe this side of idiosyncratic.

This is the one chapter in which I can tyrannically say that there is only one right way to do things. In discussing how you should dress for an interview, I feel entirely comfortable throwing impartiality and individualism out the window. Once you're in the interview, you will be playing the interviewer's game. If you want the job, you must play by her rules.

How men should dress for the interview

There is no magic or imagination required to pick out the best outfit a man should wear on a job interview—just make like Betsy Ross and think red, white, and blue. Red tie, white shirt, blue suit.

Invest now in a navy blue wool, wool-worsted, or wool-blend suit. It will look better and last longer than a suit made of other fabrics, and it will go with almost anything. Select a single-breasted, two-piece fashion, preferably vented.

This might sound old-fashioned, but for most jobs, your best bet is to dress conservatively, with minimal flash. Your shirt should be long-sleeved, professionally starched and pressed and reveal no fraying at the collar or cuffs. Button-down Oxford or spread collars are best.

Your tie should be a silk foulard in a subdued red with a stripe or small pattern in the same blue as your suit.

Remember that you should not wear any pins, cuff links, or ties that bear a religious or service affiliation (unless you want to make your outside affiliation a basis for your employment). Why risk turning an interviewer off?

One possible exception might arise if you discover through your research that you share a common affiliation with your interviewer. In this case, for example, wearing a subtle Masonic pin might make a positive impression on an interviewer who's a mason. The danger, even in this case, is that you will so impress the interviewer that he will bring you around to meet some other people who *don't* share that affiliation. In general, it's better to avoid the outer display. If you've discovered something you have in common, simply work it into your conversation in a diplomatic and natural way.

Your watch should not be a Swatch or other stylish plastic make, but a conservative model with a stretch metal or leather band—it needn't be expensive.

Wear black or navy blue socks that cover your entire calf. If you cross your legs during the interview, you don't want any of your rugby injuries to show.

And don't forget to polish your shoes. They should be black, conservative loafers or lace-ups with a low heel.

How women should dress for the interview

As you'll notice throughout your career, women have a great deal more flexibility than men in their choice of business attire. However, the greater number of options doesn't grant women complete freedom in an interview situation.

Women must take care to avoid what could be considered provocative clothing—V-neck sweaters, short skirts, or patterned stockings, for example. They should wear dresses or suits in muted colors and non-shiny fabrics.

Women should also avoid large, clunky, or noisy fashion jewelry, oversized hand-bags, open-toed shoes, and spiked heels. You'll want to look much more like Ally McBeal than Julia Roberts in *Pretty Woman*.

Unisex grooming for success

There are several grooming rules that apply to both sexes:

- **Don't overdo the perfume or cologne.** It's not that you shouldn't wear perfume or cologne, but don't wear so much that your "essence" lingers in the room for the rest of the week.

- **Carry a slim, easy-to-carry leather folder**— just large enough to hold a few copies of your resume and a small notebook.

- **Pay attention to hygiene and grooming.** Your hair (including mustaches and beards, men) should be neatly trimmed. Avoid excessive hair spray and, if possible, the types of hairstyles that require it. Make sure that your fingernails are clean and clipped. Women should avoid dark or red nail polish. And don't have any spicy foods on the way to the appointment.

If you smoke, avoid doing so prior to the interview. Virtually all workplaces are "smoke-free" these days. The smell of "eau de smoke" on your clothes will indicate you may have a problem following an important company policy.

Watch your (body) language

You'll have so much to think about during the interview that you might well overlook what your body is up to. I watched a candidate pick at a mole during an entire 45-minute interview, oblivious to how uncomfortable this might make even the most stout-hearted (and strong-stomached) interviewer, of which I was not one. Here are some tips that will keep your body from betraying you.

Hands off!

When you get to the reception area, take off your coat and hat and hang them in a closet, if one is available. This will ensure that you have one less thing to fumble with later on. If you are in the reception area for a while, keep your hands exposed, not in your pockets. This will keep them from getting too clammy.

When the interviewer comes to meet you, extend your hand, look him straight in the eye, and offer a greeting. Make sure that your handshake is firm, but not crushing, and don't worry about your palms being a little damp. Most interviewers understand that this is not an easy moment for any candidate.

Follow the interviewer into his office. This is a good time to make some small talk. "My, these offices are beautiful! How long have you been at this address?" Or, "We're lucky to have such cool weather in August (or such warm weather in November), aren't we?"

Remember, try to keep your conversation positive. It's a bad idea to start off with something like, "Boy, I can't stand this muggy weather," Or, "I thought I would never find this place!" You may prompt the interviewer to think, at least on a subconscious level, that you're a negative person or that you secretly wished you were somewhere else.

Sitting pretty

As you enter the interviewer's office, wait for his cue before you sit. If you are offered a choice, choose the chair closest to and directly opposite the interviewer's. This will demonstrate your confidence.

Don't immediately begin rooting around in your folder for your resume. Let a little more small talk help you—and the interviewer—ease into the Q & A.

Again, the conversational icebreaker should be fairly innocuous, but upbeat: "How many employees do you have here at headquarters?" "This part of the state sure has seen a lot of development recently, hasn't it?"

If you are seated at a table, interlock your fingers and keep your hands on the tabletop. This will keep you from fidgeting. If seated on a chair or couch, keep your feet flat on the floor (don't cross your legs), your hands in your lap, and interlock your fingers.

This is not to say that you shouldn't talk with your hands if you're like me and do so quite naturally. Be yourself—but when you're not using your hands to make a point, it's best to keep them folded and still.

Make eye contact throughout the entire interview, but don't overdo it. You're not engaged in a staring contest with Clint Eastwood. And staring without pause at the interviewer will not make his day.

Be aware of your body. Take care not to slouch—you may appear lazy or sloppy. On the other hand, don't sit there like a marine at attention. You're likely to seem edgy and overly aggressive—a real "Type A" personality.

A list of absolute "don'ts"

This is as good a place as any to list those mistakes that will make an average interviewer cringe and a busy interviewer simply suggest you try another company. These are the things to avoid in *any* interview or in the answer to *any* question:

- ◆ Poor grooming.
- ◆ Showing up late.
- ◆ Inappropriate dress.

- An answer, good and specific or not, that simply does not answer the question asked.
- Defensiveness, especially if it's about something that doesn't appear to need defending.
- Lack of knowledge of the company, job, and/or industry (evidence of poor or nonexistent preparation and research).
- Dishonesty.
- Lack of enthusiasm/interest.
- Asking the wrong questions.
- Any answer that reveals you are clearly unqualified for the job.
- Any disparity between your resume/cover letter and interview answers (such as providing details about jobs not on your resume).
- Lack of focus.
- Lack of eye contact.
- Any negativity, especially in discussing people (your last boss, co-workers).
- Inability to take responsibility for failures/ weaknesses/bad decisions/bad results, or taking credit for what clearly was contributed to by others.

Although most interviewers will not consider most of these an automatic reason for dismissal, an accumulation of two or more may force even the most empathetic to question your suitability. (Some items, of course, such as dishonesty, may well lead to an immediate and heartfelt "thank you...see you.")

Are you nervous?

If you have a pulse, of course you are! The interview is a difficult situation, but you can't allow nervousness to make you freeze. Here are some additional tips on relaxing so that you'll be at your best during the interview:

- ✦ **Take a deep breath.** In fact, take several while you're waiting for the interviewer to greet you. This will help stem the natural "fight-or-flight" response we all experience when we're anxious. Deep breathing helps even the worst phobics control their fears. It's an effective way to overcome the physiological causes of panic.

- ✦ **Do a last-minute check.** Make sure that your resume is readily available in your folder. Then, pick up a magazine and read the most meaningless article you can find. But avoid newspapers— the newsprint probably will come off on your sweaty palms.

- ✦ **Think about what you're here to learn.** The interviewer is not the only one seeking information. You have come to this interview to find out more about the company. So think of yourself as an important participant in the interview, not just one of many interchangeable candidates to be studied like a specimen on a slide. In fact, *you* will be in charge of some parts of the interview. So get ready to speak up.

Think of the interview as an adventure, as a learning experience, as a chance to brag about yourself, and actually (or hopefully) get rewarded for it.

Don't get off to a bad start

All of this advice is fairly easy to remember. Your choice of wardrobe is limited. And you have to remember to be enthusiastic, polite, and calm. However, following the advice can be a bit more difficult when your heart is beating like mad as you head to the interviewer's office.

Practice deep breathing—that's right, practice it—so that it comes easily and automatically when stress begins to set in. Have one of your friends or relatives play the role of the Grand Inquisitor so you can rehearse how you will act during the interview. If you have access to the equipment, videotape a role-play interview. You'll notice little tics and habits that you might be able to control so they don't distract the interviewer from the person encased in that nice blue suit.

Now that you're well dressed and ready, let's get on to the real thing.

Chapter 7

Your Interview With the Hiring Manager

Right now you're probably thinking, "Hey, I'll be doing really well if I make it past the screener in the human resources department who has been trained in this interviewing stuff. The hiring manager probably doesn't know as much about interviewing, so getting past him will be a piece of cake."

Wrong!

Skilled interviewers—those conducting the screening interviews—have had ample experience with the interview process. They are ready with a set of questions. And unless you turn them off in the first few minutes, they will proceed to ask each one.

They know how to stay in charge of an interview, not let it meander down some dead-end sidetrack.

And they usually won't ask any questions they aren't legally permitted to.

In other words, they know what they're doing and how to do it. And they are confident in their skills and knowledge. Ironically, this makes them *easier* to interview with than hiring managers.

Almost surely, hiring managers will lack some or all of the screening interviewers' knowledge, experience, and interviewing skills. Therefore, they pose a much greater challenge. The hiring manager is more likely to ask open-ended questions, more likely to lose control of the interview, and more prone to meander. In many ways, you'll be on your own, in uncharted waters, much like the early explorers sailing into territory noted on maps as, "Here there be dragons."

Your goal during the interview with the hiring manager is to inspire her confidence in you. That means you will have to be more prepared.

Flying by the seats of their pants

Why are hiring managers, for the most part, inferior interviewers? Because very few managers in corporate America actually know what it takes to hire the right candidate. Most of them have never had formal training in conducting an interview.

What's more, most managers conducting interviews are only slightly more comfortable than the candidates sitting opposite them.

Many hiring managers lack confidence, or possess only false confidence, about their ability to conduct a penetrating, conclusive interview. Why is this potentially dangerous to you? Well, it could mean that he will decide you are not the best candidate after asking vague questions or even *wrong* questions. In other words, the person who interviews you might make a hiring decision based on factors that have virtually little or nothing to do with you or your actual qualifications!

Just as the screening interviewer is looking for a set of facts that will help her give candidates a "pass" or "fail" grade, the hiring manager is looking for insights into the personality of the candidate.

He is looking for just enough information to allow intuition to take over. In other words, facts are often not the goal. The hiring manager is looking for a candidate she can feel good about hiring. That places the focus of the interview not only on your measurable skills, but on something much more subjective— her sense of whether you are likely to be a good "organizational fit."

Of course, some hiring managers are skilled interviewers. These are the people who will use techniques such as the situational interview to get a sense of how a candidate will perform on the job. Those who lack skills (the majority) tend to be much more passive. Many are secretly hoping that the candidate will do a certain "something" during the interview that will be the equivalent of saying, "Hey, I'm the one for you."

In this chapter, the most important in the book, I'll discuss how to inspire the hiring manager, how to field questions such as, "So, tell me about yourself," and how to know when it's appropriate for you to seize control of the interview.

Inspiring confidence

How can you convey your confidence and enthusiasm to a hiring manager? Here are some tips:

- **Think of the interview as an adventure.** I know that might sound strange, but you *can* make even the toughest interview an enjoyable experience if you display enthusiasm and get the hiring manager interested in you.

- **Be polite.** You may need to be tactful during the interview. For instance, if the interviewer says something you deem offensive, don't overreact. Just pause a moment and say, "Well, I know many people feel that way, but I think..." In other words, be a diplomat.

- **Be enthusiastic.** About the position, about your accomplishments, about what you've found out about the company. I remember one candidate who sat like a bump on a log throughout an interview for a junior editorial position. She asked no questions and gave only terse replies to mine. I cut the interview short because I felt she didn't want the job. I was shocked when she repeatedly called to see if I'd made my final choice. It turned out that she *desperately* wanted the position. She certainly didn't convey that to me when it really *counted*.

- **Keep on smiling.** A smile makes you appear agreeable and pleasant. And who wouldn't want to work with a pleasant and agreeable person like you? Your smiles should be natural, spontaneous and, most of all, sincere.

- **Make eye contact.** Have you ever known someone who wouldn't look you in the eye? Eventually, you began to wonder what that person had to hide. Make eye contact while you're shaking hands with the interviewer and periodically throughout the interview. But avoid staring or making continuous eye contact—that would make anyone feel uncomfortable.

- **Be honest.** Express enthusiasm only about the things you are truly enthusiastic about. Don't gush.

- **Be positive.** It's best to keep negative words out of your interview vocabulary. If you switched majors and the interviewer asks why, don't say, "I couldn't stand the professors in the economics department. I just had to get out of there." Instead, try something like, "I got a lot out of studying economics, but I became absolutely fascinated with marketing, so I decided to make the switch." As you rehearse your answers to interview questions, eliminate *all* of the negative words.

- **Don't let an unskilled interviewer torpedo your chances.** Your advance preparation should give you the power to take control of the interview, allowing you to emphasize the many ways you can contribute to the company.

"So, tell me a little about yourself."

This is the favorite question of the trained interviewer, because it gives him the opportunity to study a host of reactions—from verbal cues to body language.

It is also a favorite of the *un*trained interviewer for quite a different reason—because he usually doesn't know what else to ask.

Therefore, it's a good idea to assume that this question—or a variation thereof—will be one of the first asked, if not *the* first. Prepare for it the way presidential candidates prepare for televised debates—by developing and rehearsing a set reply. Otherwise, you may be fated to react like the narrator in essayist J. B. Priestly's piece, "All About Ourselves":

> *"Now tell me," said the lady, "all about your-self." The effect was instantaneous, shattering. Up to that moment, I had been feeling expansive; I was self-confident, alert, ready to give a good account of myself in the skirmish of talk. If I had been asked my opinion of anything between here and Sirius, I would have given it at length, and I was quite prepared to talk of places I had never seen and books I had never read; I was ready to lie, and to lie boldly and well. Had she not made that fatal demand, I would have roared.*

When *you* are asked this "killer" question, remember the cardinal rule of interviewing: The hiring manager wants to feel good about you. Your primary goal is to let him do just that.

And there is a second rule: The hiring manager wants you to make him feel confident that hiring you will be a good decision. Your answer to this question should be targeted to do just that.

Taking stock once again

To prepare an excellent answer to this question, look back at the personal inventory I urged you to prepare in Chapter 1.

Most important in preparing your answer are items you listed under the headings:

- Strongest skills.

- Greatest areas of knowledge.

- Strongest parts of personality.

- Things I do best.

- Key accomplishments.

From this information, you will now construct a well-thought-out, logically sequenced summary of your experience, skills, talents, and schooling. A plus? If this brief introduction clearly and succinctly ties your experience into the requirements of the position. But be sure to keep it tightly focused—about 250 to 350 words, chock-full of specifics. It should take you no more than two minutes to recite an answer that includes the following information:

- Brief introduction.

- Key accomplishments.

- Key strengths demonstrated by these accomplishments.

- Importance of these strengths and accomplishments to the prospective employer.

- Where and how you see yourself developing in the position for which you're applying (tempered with the right amount of self-deprecating humor and modesty).

Again, we're not talking *War and Peace* here. Two-hundred-fifty to 350 words is about right (taking from 90 to 120 seconds to recite).

Here's how Barb, a recent college graduate applying for an entry-level sales position, answered these questions:

I've always been able to get along with different types of people. I think it's because I'm a good talker and an even better listener. (Modestly introduces herself, while immediately laying claim to the most important skills a good salesperson should have.)

During my senior year in high school, when I began thinking seriously about which careers I'd be best suited for, sales came to mind almost immediately. In high school and during my summer breaks from college, I worked various part-time jobs at retail outlets. (Demonstrates industriousness and at least some related experience.) *Unlike most of my friends, I actually liked dealing with the public.* (Conveys enthusiasm for selling.)

However, I also realized that retail had its limitations, so I went on to read about other types of sales positions. I was particularly fascinated by what is usually described as consultative selling. I like the idea of going to a client you have really done your homework on and showing him how your products can help him solve one of his nagging problems, and then following through on that. (Shows interest and enthusiasm for the job.)

After I wrote a term paper on consultative selling in my senior year of college, I started looking for companies at which I could learn and refine the skills shared by people who are working as account executives. (Shows initiative both in researching the area of consultative selling to write a term paper and in then researching prospective companies.)

That led me to your company, Mr. Sheldon. I find the prospect of working with companies to increase the energy efficiency of their installations exciting. I've also learned some things about your sales training programs. They sound like they're on the cutting edge. (Gives evidence that she is an enthusiastic self-starter.)

I guess the only thing I find a little daunting about the prospect of working at Co-generation, Inc., is selling that highly technical equipment without a degree in engineering. By the way, what sort of support does your technical staff lend to the sales effort? (Demonstrates that she is willing to learn what she doesn't know and closes by deferring to the interviewer's authority. By asking a question the interviewer must answer, Barb has also given herself a little breather. Now the conversational ball sits squarely in the interviewer's court.)

Based on the apparent sincerity and detail of her answers, it's not a bad little "speech" of a mere 253 words, is it?

Write your little speech on a piece of paper, rewrite it, rewrite it—then rewrite it again. You want it to sound natural and conversational, but to include all the key points you want to emphasize.

It should not have a lot of dependent clauses and tricky constructions, because people don't talk that way unless they've memorized a speech. You *don't* want to sound like Jerry Seinfeld reading from internal cue cards. That would certainly give the interviewer a bad impression. But if you have a speech like the one above, you'll knock him out.

Also, anticipate the questions the interviewer might ask after you give your speech about yourself and prepare answers for *those* questions. You certainly don't want to look as if you have nothing more to say after you've finished your canned presentation.

Taking control of the interview

Many candidates go into the interview thinking they are there for only one reason: to answer questions.

Nothing could be further from the truth. Yes, you are going to the interview for only one reason, but that reason is *to sell the interviewer on the fact that you are the best person for the job.*

You will do this by *giving* terrific answers to the interviewer's questions, by *asking* great questions about the company and the position, and by *telling* the interviewer the things about yourself that you want him or her to know.

Let's say you went to an automobile showroom knowing just a little about a particular car. You are approached by an affable salesman who answers your questions but doesn't volunteer any information and asks no questions of you. Do you think you'd end up buying a car from him?

Most candidates approach the job interview like this hapless salesman. They are prepared to answer questions, but hesitate to volunteer information unless it's asked for—even if that information concerns some of their key talents or strengths.

Don't miss the opportunity to sell yourself. The fact that a customer walked into the showroom should have been enough to inspire that car salesman to do his best. Similarly, the fact that you've been called in for the interview has given you a chance to sell yourself. Don't blow it just because the interviewer doesn't ask the questions you were hoping he would. Find some way to give your answers anyway.

Seize the day

Many less-experienced interviewers have a tendency to talk too much. In those situations, you must take charge—ask questions constantly.

If the interviewer has been speaking nonstop for 10 minutes when he says, "We've increased sales 20 percent every year for the past decade," politely interrupt with a question like, "That's very impressive in a mature industry like yours. How has the company maintained such growth?"

At the opposite extreme is the interviewer who will let the poor candidate ramble on and on in answer to a single question because he has so few others to ask.

If you're faced with such a situation, watch how the interviewer is reacting to your soliloquy. If he exhibits what seems to be a negative response—crossing his arms across his chest, sitting bolt upright in his chair, fidgeting, tapping his fingers on the desk, shuffling papers—change the subject or ask him a question. You're not getting anywhere by continuing to flap your gums.

Don't make the mistake of talking faster once you notice his discomfort. You may be thinking this will help you get to whatever the interviewer really wants to hear faster. It's more likely that he just wants to hear his own voice for a minute or two!

I'll discuss interview questions and answers at greater length in Chapter 9. For now, just remember that the interview with the hiring manager is apt to be quite different from that with the human resources department. But if you handle it correctly, it also presents a greater opportunity to allow your key strengths to shine through.

Again, I urge you to be prepared with a little speech about who you are, and to be ready to answer a far greater number of open-ended questions (starting with why and how, rather than who, what, and where).

If you want to use your school experiences as a reference, think of the HR department interviews as the multiple-choice and true/false parts of the exam, while the hiring manager's interview is more like the essay section. You have to know the facts for both, but the second requires you to explain the implications of those facts.

Also remember that, unlike the screening interviewer, the hiring manager's primary goal in an interview is to establish not a set of facts, but a feeling. She wants to feel confident that you are the best person for the job. Don't let a lack of preparation or a hesitancy to speak up keep you from a job you want and deserve.

Chapter 8

The Finer Points of Interview Technique

Until now, I've discussed, in broad strokes, how you should conduct yourself during the interview. In this chapter, I'll present some of the finer points that will help you score big when you meet with the HR department or the hiring manager.

I know that it seems as if you already have a lot to think about, but some of the lessons in this chapter will really help you stand out from the crowd of candidates.

Demonstrate an interest in the interviewer

Surprisingly enough, interviewers *are* human (for the most part). Like you, they respond positively to people who demonstrate a genuine interest in them. And they become impatient or bored with people who seem self-absorbed.

So you can score big points if you demonstrate an interest in the interviewer. This is particularly true if the interview is with the hiring manager. After all, she is looking for an individual whose mission will be to help her, someone attentive and responsive. Showing an interest in her will go a long way toward convincing her that you will care about her needs and goals after you're hired.

A friend of mine landed a prime position at a brand-new company launched by a legendary entrepreneur in his industry. He was selected over many good candidates for this plum position. This was a triumph for my friend, especially since this entrepreneur, whom I'll call Larry, was known to be difficult to impress.

My friend, Cameron, told this story about the interview:

Here was Larry, a multimillionaire, sitting with a secretary and one other employee in this nearly empty 10,000 square feet of office shell. They had lights, a phone, a postage machine, some furniture, and that's about it. There were workmen off in one corner, building some walls for his office.

Naturally, I was expecting a little more, and somehow these strange circumstances completely wiped away my nervousness. When Larry stood up to greet me, I introduced myself, then said, "I bet it has been a long time since you opened your own mail." At first, I couldn't believe I had done that, but Larry laughed and off we went.

For the next hour, Cameron had a ball talking with Larry about the launch of what promised to be an exciting company. He stayed loose during the entire interview, realizing that his going out on a limb had paid off. He felt—and expressed—enthusiasm for the utter lack of structure at the new company and said, "Larry really picked up on that. I could sense his violent dislike for big structures, so I took pains to stress *my* preference for lean, mean companies."

Cameron's move was risky. In this case, it worked because it displayed confidence, it implied knowledge of Larry's background and it suggested that Cameron was aware that Larry wanted this company to grow to the point that a mailroom would make sense.

Cameron had a great deal of control in the interview because he continued to demonstrate an interest in Larry's problems. In fact, in response to almost any of the challenges Larry discussed, Cameron had a question. Cameron came across as an interested, sympathetic problem-solver. He got an offer for the job that afternoon.

Granted, Cameron was presented with a golden interview opportunity. But he had the experience—and the *chutzpah*— to seize upon it and play it to the hilt.

Oh, sure you can!

You're probably saying, "But I can't do anything like *that*." Maybe not. It's not often that opportunities like the one Cameron had come along. What's more, you don't have the type of job experience he had to wow an interviewer.

But you *can* display your interest in the interviewer with the simplest of comments: "I recognized you from your picture in the employee newsletter. Congratulations on your recent promotion." "That's a wonderful photograph on your wall. Where was it taken?"

Build a vocabulary of positive action words

What? A vocabulary lesson for a 45-minute interview?

Granted, this might seem like overkill, but you'll use this vocabulary on your resume, in your job-hunting letters, during interviews, in your follow-up letters—and in every business letter you'll write for the rest of your life.

Always think in terms of positive, action words. They needn't be "five-dollar" words, but they should be words that stand out from normal conversational lingo. The list on page 117 is just a sample, but you get the idea.

Read it over every day. Utilize them in the little speech about yourself discussed in the last chapter.

Action Words

accomplished	edited	obtained
achieved	eliminated	operated
accelerated	established	ordered
administered	evaluated	organized
analyzed	examined	performed
approved	formulated	planned
arranged	founded	prepared
assisted	guided	presented
built	headed	produced
calculated	identified	provided
compiled	implemented	recommended
completed	improved	reduced
composed	increased	reorganized
conducted	initiated	replaced
consolidated	inspected	reported
consulted	installed	researched
controlled	instituted	reviewed
coordinated	instructed	revised
created	invented	scheduled
decreased	justified	selected
delivered	led	solved
designed	lectured	studied
developed	maintained	supervised
devised	managed	trained
directed	modified	translated
discovered	motivated	won
distributed	negotiated	wrote

Concentrate, concentrate, concentrate

Have you ever been in a conversation and realized that while you've been speaking, the person supposedly listening to you was thinking only about what he'd say next? You'd probably think that person was pretty self-centered and obviously uninterested in you and what you had to say.

Employers go one step further. They think that people demonstrating such behavior during a job interview are lacking one of the most important skills a good employee needs: the ability to listen, to be attentive, to react to the situation at hand.

During an interview, many candidates have a tendency to let their guard down after a certain amount of time. Oh, they start off enthusiastically and attentively, full of vim and vigor, but once they think they've gotten through the toughest part of the interview, they start to relax.

Don't do it. Don't get *too* relaxed. You should be concentrating on everything the interviewer says and asks so that you can formulate impressive questions and tell him precisely what he wants to know.

I know that you're at a time in your life when staying up late is the norm. Before the big day of your job interview, pack it in early. Get plenty of rest so you're ready to face this big challenge alert and at your best.

Unless you have an adverse reaction to caffeine, have a cup or two of coffee or tea about 30 minutes before the interview. Just don't overdo it—a fidgety caffeine overdose is hell to deal with during an interview!

Answer the question

After you give an answer, look your interviewer in the eye and prepare to listen, and I mean *listen*, to the next question. Then give him the appropriate answer.

If the interviewer asked for a specific set of facts, don't lose yourself in a mountain of detail and conjure up all of the implications and explanations he didn't ask for.

Be terse and direct. You'll score more points. Long-winded answers will make the interviewer wish you'd go bend some other manager's ear.

Many interviewees seem to be under the false assumption that they will score extra points during their interviews if they answer questions quickly. So, they begin speaking as soon as the interviewer finishes with the question, usually rushing headlong into an answer they soon wish they could revise or, worse yet, withdraw entirely!

It's a much better idea to allow for a short pause after the question so that you can compose a terrific answer.

What if a short pause is not enough? Then stall for more time with phrases like "Now, let me see," or, "I'm glad you asked that question." Or paraphrase the question:

> **Interviewer:** *Tell me, what made you decide to change your major six times during your undergraduate days?*
>
> **Candidate:** *Why did I change my major so often? Well, let me see, there were several reasons while I was an underclassman, but...*

See? Without a lot of "umms" and "uhhs," the candidate has successfully stalled for time.

No question is a throwaway

Some questions might seem unimportant, but don't ever treat them that way. Give equally careful consideration to every answer.

For instance, one acquaintance of mine thought that enthusiasm and a good work ethic should weigh more heavily in his consideration of candidates for most positions than their experience or education.

So many of the seemingly innocent questions he asked were designed to evaluate to what degree candidates possessed these characteristics. He asked about hobbies, believing that those without outside interests were either dull or lazy.

He'd also give careful consideration to candidates' comments about the weather, getting to the interview, the hectic days after college.

Candidates who consistently expressed negative views or started whining about these matters were not considered for hire.

So be on your guard—remember that most employers are looking for enthusiasm, confidence, dependability, and vigor.

If you whine your way through questions about the weather, you won't be thought of as someone possessing energy and the right attitude.

And if you point out that it took you hours to find the interviewer's office because you failed to get detailed directions, well, so much for your competence and dependability.

Be decisive

Open-ended questions are a double-edged sword. In Chapter 6, I urged you to prepare a little speech to deliver when you're asked, "So, tell me about yourself."

Well, there are a lot of other open-ended questions likely to come up:

- What are your key strengths?
- What are your goals?
- What accomplishments are you most proud of?
- Why did you choose your major?
- Why do you want to relocate to our area?
- How would your best friend describe you?

You should have prepared the answers to these and similar kinds of questions.

Avoid the kinds of answers too many candidates give to these types of questions: "Boy, that's a tough one. Hmmm, I've never thought about that, but I guess if I had to choose one accomplishment, I would have to say that it might be making the dean's list seven straight semesters. Although I am really proud of my Eagle Scout pin. No, I'd have to say the dean's list. No, no, definitely the Eagle Scout pin."

Such answers make candidates look indecisive—not exactly a trait employers are looking for. So after pausing to consider your answer and stalling smoothly, hit the interviewer with your best shot—and stick with it.

Don't add, "Well, gee, maybe neither was really the one I'm most proud of. Maybe it's the fact that I earned a lot of my college expenses during my summers." Sure, you want to score that point, but wait for another opportunity.

The sounds of silence

Nothing sounds worse to a stand-up comic than silence. Hence, the old line, "I know you're out there. I can hear you breathing," from the comedian desperate for a laugh.

If the silence starts to become deafening during your interview, you'll probably feel even more desperate. And that's just how some interviewers want you to feel. The most experienced inquisitors use silence to see how a candidate will squirm. And squirm they usually do!

A candidate confronted by interviewer silence will begin retracting what he just said, restating what he just said in slightly different words, or volunteering more information than he should. Not helpful reactions.

Avoid doing any of these things. My best advice is the same given to every neophyte sales representative: "Once you've made the sale, shut up." (Granted, it's the lesson that takes most salespeople a lifetime to learn.)

Retracting, restating, muttering, or launching into a complete history of your life when you're faced with interviewer silence will not help your image at all. It will make you appear indecisive.

Or, worse, it might lead you to say things you'd decided you wouldn't say during the interview—the less-than-rational reasons you switched majors, the fact that you hated your internships, or that you were rejected by seven graduate schools. When you are finished answering a question, *show* you are done—meet the interviewer's silence with some confident silence of your own. Then, break it with a question so that, once again, you can feel in control of the interview.

Don't worry, be positive

Go into the interview thinking, "I am going to get this job." If you want the job, go into the interview with the attitude that it's yours for the taking. Don't be cocky, but do be confident. Express your enthusiasm for the job and for the opportunity to be considered for it. And be positive about everything, even the weather.

Think of the type of people you would like to work with. They are happy to be on the job, bright, willing to help. Your goal is to convince the interviewer that she would like to work with *you.*

Special tips for recent college grads

- ◆ Don't be afraid to say you'll need help. And when you do need help, make sure that the interviewer knows you'll ask for it. Not many companies are looking for—or expect to find—a 22-year-old know-it-all. If you *are* a 22-year-old know-it-all, keep it to yourself.

- ◆ Admit that you don't have all the answers. Begin a lot of your answers with "I think..." or "From what I know about the industry..."

- ◆ Don't appear squeamish at the idea of going through the school of hard knocks. Tell the interviewer, "Sure, I know this position has its share of unpleasant duties, but I'm sure everyone who's had this job before me has learned a lot by doing them."

- There are interviewers out there—and I'm one of them—that go out of their way to describe in excruciating detail the worst or most mind-numbingly boring aspects of a job. Don't be fooled into expressing *any* negative reaction (even a raised eyebrow when "garbage detail" is being discussed).

- If it took a while for you to find your direction, admit it. Nobody has all the answers at 18 or 19. How many people know from the start that they wanted to be accountants or hospital administrators? Most interviewers will not be surprised that you changed majors as an undergraduate. Show how your other studies contributed to making you the best candidate.

- Don't answer any question about who paid for your educational expenses or about any outstanding educational loans you may be carrying. Go ahead and play up the fact that you received a full academic scholarship or were industrious enough to work your way through school, if you want to. But by law, you don't have to say any more. For more detail on how to recognize and deflect illegal questions, see Chapter 10.

Chapter 9

How to Answer the Toughest Questions

Like television plots, all interview questions fall into roughly three groups:

1. Factual questions about your education and job experience.

2. Questions designed to determine who you really are and what you're made of.

3. Questions that will help the interviewer predict how you might perform on the job.

In the preceding chapters, I've discussed, in a general way, how you will answer these questions. This chapter presents the questions you should expect to confront somewhere along the line, with some discussion of what the interviewer is seeking to learn and how you should answer each one. (For a much more detailed discussion of these questions and answers, I suggest my other interviewing book, *101 Great Answers to the Toughest Interview Questions*.)

You should *not* spend time preparing answers to all of these questions in advance, writing them down, and memorizing them. If you did that, you might not go on your first interview until you were eligible for Medicare. But you should have the necessary facts to answer them in some relatively retrievable portion of your brain.

Your education and experience

Here's a basic list of questions about your education and experience you should expect to be asked during your first interview:

1. What extracurricular activities did you participate in? What made you choose those activities? Which of them did you most enjoy? Why?

2. Did you hold any leadership positions while you were in college? What do you think you learned?

3. What did you learn from the (or, Why don't I see any) internships on your resume? How did you get them?

4. What were the most valuable lessons you learned from your part-time job(s)?

5. If you were to start college over again tomorrow, what courses would you take? Why?

6. What sort of grades did you get in your major? In your minor? In what courses did you get your best grades? Why? In what courses did you get your worst grades? Why? How do you think that will affect your performance on the job?

7. What were the factors that led you to select your college?

8. What led you to choose that major over others?

9. What type of student were you?

10. Which courses did you like the most? Why? Which courses did you like the least? Why?

11. What are your most memorable experiences from college?

12. Why did you (or didn't you) decide to go to graduate school?

13. Why are you applying for a job in a field other than your major?

14. Were there any unusual difficulties you had to overcome to do so well in college? How did you do it?

15. What did you spend most of your time doing during your internship(s)?

These questions might seem prosaic enough, but they all have a hidden agenda. The interviewer is really probing to determine how ambitious and "trainable" you are.

No company really believes that someone is going to come out of college or graduate school and be productive immediately. Many are willing (and expect) to invest in training you to "forget what you learned in school and learn how to do things the *right* way," even if that takes months.

The interviewer, therefore, is actually probing to see whether you're a know-it-all or sensible enough to know you still have a lot to learn and to determine the extent to which you've been pampered—used to having things go your way with very little effort on your part.

Your major

When discussing your major, it's a good idea to be decisive, to say that you are convinced you chose the right field, even though it might have taken you a while to find it: "I'm really glad I majored in Pseudoscience. I only wish that I had known a little more about it when I began my studies. I could have taken a couple of other courses in the discipline as an undergraduate."

Be prepared to explain how and why you made certain decisions. Did you choose that major because it was the easiest? Because it was relevant to other interests, which your volunteer and work experience clearly support? Because you took courses to prepare for a particular career? Because you had to choose something?

What other major or minors did you consider? And why did you choose one over another?

If you changed majors, be ready to explain why. Don't worry—none of us were *that* together when we were 19. Most interviewers will not consider it a negative if can you coherently explain *why*. They're more interested in your thought process than the actual facts—*unless* you blame someone or something else for your decision. *That* will lead to a host of questions you *don't* want them asking...or even thinking: Do you have a problem with authority? Are you unwilling to take responsibility for your own decisions? Are you still immature?

The less your major has to do with the job for which you're applying, the more explaining you will have to do. Keep your answer brief but positive: You reexamined your career goals. You identified interests, skills, or talents you didn't even know about when you chose your major. And by gosh, who would have ever thought actuarial work could be so darned exciting!

Your grades

Many companies will ask to see copies of college transcripts, so you may as well come clean now. If you flunked every accounting course and have even a modicum of intelligence, you're probably not applying for an accounting job, right? Hopefully you can blame the bad grades you received in some of your electives on the amount of time and effort you were putting into your major.

While interviewers will not expect everyone to graduate with straight As, they will be understandably dubious of a C or D student's application. *There must be some explanation*—or you won't be considered for virtually any job. Period.

Your coursework

"Which courses did you like best?" Concentrate on the skills you developed in some of your courses—writing ability, debating skills, language skills—that will serve you well in this job. When naming your favorite courses or talking about your most memorable experiences, focus on those that are career-oriented, assuming you took courses related to the job at hand.

When asked about your least favorite courses, of course you will pick one *not* related to your eventual career. Try to develop answers that have to do with the *subject*, rather than such things as the professor's personality or the workload.

I personally like to hear that a candidate did well in a course she didn't really like, even one she didn't want to take at all. There are all too many times, whatever your job or profession, that you will have to do something simply because it has to be done. Demonstrating that you are capable of doing good work even when bored to tears is a plus.

Some interviewers may try to trick you by asking, "What college professors did you most enjoy? Why?" They're still trying to find out how you think and make decisions. In this case, make sure your answer concentrates on what you learned, not which professor was the most entertaining.

Changes you'd make

What would you do differently if you were starting college today? Think about changes you would make in your course selection that would have made you a better candidate for *the job you're seeking*. Should you have taken more marketing courses, an accounting course, or statistics seminar?

Be candid—you can freely admit that in hindsight, at least, your choices were not always as wise as you would have liked. But don't go over the edge and proclaim yourself ready to change colleges, major, minor, and hair color.

You have been given the opportunity to show how much you know about the job for which you're applying—make sure your answer reflects that knowledge.

Why didn't you enroll in graduate school? You were chomping at the bit to get out into the real world, to start working at a company like this one. Graduate degrees are not necessary for every profession, of course. But even if you are planning to earn your M.B.A. some time in the future, there's nothing wrong with wanting to get some work experience first.

Extracurricular activities

So you haven't run up a huge list of extracurricular accomplishments because you really had to hit the books to get good grades. If the interviewer asks, "Why didn't you get more involved in outside activities?" don't reply, "Oh, I spent a lot of time studying and I didn't want those things to get in the way of my social life." (Or, worse, "Well, I was too darned busy drinking beer and chasing girls.")

Instead, say something like, "I got involved in a few things. I wish I had done more, but I really was interested in my studies. I cracked the books every night; that's what enabled me to finish second in the class."

It's always a good idea to portray yourself as a well-rounded person. If your weren't a member of many official school clubs or teams, talk about other activities you engaged in during college. Did you tutor other students? Work to gain extra course credit? But be careful: If you boast of a plethora of outside activities but sport a woeful GPA, the interviewer will naturally wonder why you spent so little time concentrating on your schoolwork.

A friend of mine had to work his way through college, holding down a number of menial positions totally unrelated to the career he hoped eventually to enter. He simply could not afford to be on low-paying internships during his summers or involve himself in a lot of extracurricular activities. He had to pump gas.

This presented a quandary during his interview at a publishing company, a very internship-oriented field.

My friend knew questions about these things would come up from his interviewer. Therefore, he was prepared with answers like, "I wish I'd had more time to do things like work on the school paper, but whenever I wasn't studying, I pretty much had to work to pay for college. During all of those jobs, though, I learned a number of things that people learn only after they've been in their careers for a while, like how to work with others and how to manage my time."

He turned a possible negative into a salient positive.

Needless to say, anything you've done to develop, enhance, or demonstrate leadership skills should be a primary part of your "tell me about yourself" speech and highlighted in as many answers as possible. Few companies are seeking sheep.

Internships and part-time work

Stress how the real-world experience you obtained—even if meager and short-lived—complemented the academic training you received. The more your internships or work experience tie in to the career you're supposedly seeking, the better interviewers will feel about you…and the more positively that experience will be viewed.

Be prepared for variations on these questions: "Would you repeat each of your internships? Why or why not?" "Why did you pick those particular internships?" "Why did you feel the need to do an internship?" And a good interviewer will try to unearth some facts to support your bald assertions about your performance by asking something like, "During your internships or part-time jobs, what sort of evaluations did you get from your supervisors?"

Unless you managed to land one heck of a high-flying, high-powered, part-time position—something of an oxymoron—few interviewers will actually care much about what you did, how you did it, why, who for, or with whom. They *will* be listening for some key words—those action words I listed in Chapter 8. What can you say about your internship or part-time job that shows what you accomplished, achieved, completed, discovered, initiated, performed, solved, etc.?

Open-ended questions

Don't expect every interviewer to ask pointed questions that can only be answered very narrowly. Some will delight in asking open ended questions that allow you to talk…and talk…and talk…about almost anything you want. This is *not* a good thing. You must remember that your answer to any question must highlight your strengths, illustrate your skills, and support your qualifications.

These kinds of questions can come in many shapes and sizes. Here are three examples of the many variations you may encounter:

16.   Tell me about the last time you:

- ◆   Failed.
- ◆   Succeeded.
- ◆   Made a mistake.
- ◆   Made a good decision.
- ◆   Made a poor decision.

- Failed to complete a project on time.
- Found a unique solution to a problem.
- Found a creative solution to a problem.
- Aimed too high.
- Aimed too low.

17. What do you do when you're having trouble:

- Solving a problem?
- Handling stress?
- Meeting a deadline?
- With a boss?
- With a teacher?
- With your job?
- With your school work?
- With a friend?

18. What do you do when:

- There's too much to do?
- Too little to do?
- You're tired?
- You're feeling lazy?
- You're bored?

In answering these questions, think like a writer—make sure your "story" has a beginning, middle, and end: Here's what happened, here's what I did, here's what I learned. A seasoned interviewer will use this kind of question as a launching pad for a whole series of more detailed questions designed to elicit *specific* examples to support your high-flying claims.

The more grandiose your assertions—turning that summer job stocking grocery shelves into a management position, for example—the more uncomfortable her probes will make you.

Who are you?

19. Please tell me a little bit about yourself.

20. What do you consider your key strengths?

21. What do you consider your key weaknesses? What are you planning do about them?

22. Have you ever had a weakness in the past that you've been able to overcome? How did you accomplish this?

23. Do you think that you'll prefer to work with others or by yourself? Are there experiences you have had in school or in part-time jobs that support that?

24. What do you want to accomplish in your life?

25. Which supervisor did you like the best? Why? Which did you like the least? Why?

26. Which supervisor(s) got the most out of you? Why?

27. What are some of the things you do in your spare time? What are your favorite hobbies? Do you play any sports?

28. How do you handle yourself when you're having a conflict with someone? Are you confrontational? Do you avoid that person? Why? How do you think you'll behave when you have a problem with a co-worker?

29. If you could change one thing about your personality with a snap of your fingers, what would it be? Why?

30. If I met some of your peers from college, what do you think they would say about you?

31. Would you describe yourself as a risk-taker or someone who plays it safe?

32. Why should I consider you a strong applicant for this position?

33. What's the biggest failure in your life?

34. What's the worst decision you ever made?

35. What types of people do you have trouble getting along with?

If you're hit with a series of questions like this, you'll feel like you've been put through the wringer.

Only the most annoying people *don't* find it difficult to talk about themselves in a flattering way. And that's what you'll be doing on the interview—constantly blowing your own horn until even you will want to change the tune.

You'll be saying what a great guy your friends think you are, what a pleasure your supervisors thought it was to have you on their team, that there are only a few little adjustments you'd like to make to your personality. This can all get pretty sickening.

But don't get carried away with yourself. When you're answering these questions:

 • Remember that companies are looking for these traits: enthusiasm, confidence, energy, dependability, honesty, and pride in work. Make sure you highlight specific examples from school, work, or outside activities that illustrate them.

+ Think about what you would want in an ideal employee if *you* owned a company. You'd want problem-solvers, team players, people willing to work hard, people who enjoy what they're doing, wouldn't you? So do the interviewers you'll be meeting.

+ Remember not to volunteer any negative information about yourself unless you are specifically asked for it. When you *are* asked for it, try to turn it into a positive. For example, "Well, I did have a problem with procrastination when I first entered college, but I solved it. I learned to work on my least-favorite tasks first, which made the rest of my assignments seem easy." Remember: The interviewer is not a priest, and you are not in a confessional. There is no rule requiring you to admit every horrible thing you ever did...or even one of them.

+ Let the interviewer know that you have no problem getting along with other people. However, every job situation forces us to get along with people with whom we might not choose to socialize. Acknowledge this, but talk about how you've managed to get along with a wide variety of other people.

+ On questions about self-improvement and future plans, remember that you must exhibit loyalty. Don't proclaim that you can't wait to get to graduate school to better yourself or that you hope to be in your own business in five years. Formulate answers that show you want to be in a better position *at their company* and that you're willing to accommodate *their* needs—rather than yours—first.

♦ When asked about outside activities (such as question 27), make sure you highlight those that are at least remotely job related. If you're seeking a job in publishing, your reading habits are probably pertinent. Your snowboarding skills are not.

How will you perform?

More and more employers are using "situational questions" in hopes of better predicting employee behavior on the job. These can go something like this:

36. What most influenced you to choose the career you're ready to begin?

37. When you're faced with a particularly tough decision, how do you go about making it? Can you give me an example?

38. The successful candidate for this position will be working with some highly trained individuals who have been with us for a long time. If you get the job, how will you make sure that you fit in?

39. What are you looking for in a job?

40. Let's say your supervisor gave you an assignment that you didn't understand and then left town for a week. Assume he or she is unreachable. What would you do?

41. Describe your ideal boss.

42. This is a large (or a small) company. Do you think you'd like that sort of environment? Why? What do you think you might not like about it?

43. What do you know about the financial aspects of this business? Have any of your studies or readings helped you learn about how we budget? What affects our bottom line?

44. Are you an organized person?

45. Do you manage your time well?

46. How do you handle change?

47. If your supervisor told you to do something a certain way, and you knew that way was dead wrong, what would you do?

48. You won't be managing people for a while, but if you were, how do you think your subordinates would describe you?

49. After you're on the job for a while, how do you think your co-workers will describe you?

50. Why are you interested in this position?

51. How long do you think this position will be challenging to you? What do you think you would like to do next?

52. Why this company? What about it appeals to you most?

53. Is there anything about this company or job that makes you apprehensive? Why?

54. What aspects of this job do you think you'll find the most interesting?

55. What aspects do you think you'll find the least interesting?

56. How will you react to doing the least interesting or least pleasant parts of this job?

57. How do you think this job will help you achieve your long-term career objectives?

58. Describe your ideal job based on what you know of your discipline and this industry right now.

59. How do you think the job you're applying for matches up with that description?

60. Are there any glaring shortcomings to the position based on your description of the ideal job?

61. Are you able to work overtime? On weekends?

62. Your lack of experience bothers me. Why do *you* think I should I hire someone just out of school, like you?

63. What do you want most out of your job? Money? Satisfaction? Power?

64. Can you perform well under pressure? How do you know that?

65. What does the word "success" mean to you? How about "failure"?

66. Who are our top competitors?

What they're trying this time

Most of these questions are designed to determine whether you have "organizational fit." The interviewer wants to know if you'll stick around for a while to become a valued employee, or whether the organization and/or you will soon wish you'd never heard of each other.

If you're a recent college graduate, you'll be at a distinct disadvantage in answering many of these questions. So:

- Admit when you don't have all of the answers.

- Remember the attributes the company wants most in its employees and display them every chance you get.

- Don't sound put-off by a job description that may require you to do some upleasant things.

- Be positive about your negatives.

- Don't be afraid to tell the interviewer that you'll ask for help when you need it.

- Go in prepared with this winning answer about your ideal supervisor: "The ideal supervisor has a great deal of experience in the field and enjoys delegating the challenging tasks of the department to the most deserving employees."

  "(Management expert) Peter Drucker has said that 'the manager's role is to give employees the tools they need to get the job done.' I think that's a good description of the ideal supervisor—someone who provides the resources and, when necessary, the knowledge employees need to do and enjoy their jobs."

- If you don't really know where you want to be five or more years down the road, say so in a positive way. Your answer could be something like: "Well, I loved studying biochemistry and that's why I want to work at a leading company in the field, like yours. I hope that I can learn a great deal more about the field, and that I excel enough to be given additional challenges here. I'm only sure right now that I want to work and do well in this discipline."

◆   Some of these questions are your opportunity to show off the research you've done on the company. Dazzle 'em with footwork—embellish your answers with facts about the company and the industry.

Wrapping it up

Just when you thought the grilling was over, the interviewer could very well hit you with a series of "wrap up" questions:

67. Is there anything else I should know about you?

68. Would you be willing to relocate?

69. Have you been interviewing for other positions?

70. How does this position seem to compare to others for which you've applied?

71. How long have you been looking for a job?

72. Have you received any offers? From whom? For what type of position? At what salary?

73. Why *haven't* you received any other offers?

74. When do you expect to hear from us? What is your availability?

75. What do you think of our compensation package?

76. May I contact your references?

You might not think you have anything else left to tell the interviewer, but you'd better! Here's someone giving you a chance to *close the sale.*

Develop a short answer to question 67, one that plays upon your strengths, accomplishments, skills, and areas of knowledge. For instance, "Mr. Brown, I think we've covered everything, but I want to reemphasize the key strengths that I would bring to this position," etc.

If you are interested in the position, don't be cute. Say that you are available immediately, or at least as soon as you can relocate—whatever is convenient for you and the employer. And tell the truth about other positions. You needn't bring up the names of the employers. Make it clear that the position for which you are interviewing is one you would willingly accept.

I also would advise against talking about salary at this stage. Get a sense of what the package (compensation and benefits) is, but wait until you get an offer to negotiate. That's the time when you have the most leverage.

If you're asked for references, tell the interviewer you will mail, fax, or e-mail a list of references that afternoon or, if it is already late in the day, the next morning. Be sure to notify your prospective references that a call might be coming from Mr. Brown at XYZ Company. If your references are indeed going to say wonderful things about you, they should be prepared to do so.

77.   Do you have any questions?

This is the surefire sign that the interview is drawing to a close, and if you haven't asked a question until now, it's also probably a surefire bet that you're not getting the job.

Even if you think you're sold on the position or you're clear on the responsibilities, you must speak up here. If you don't, the interviewer will assume you are uninterested. And that can be the kiss of death to you as an applicant, even at this late stage.

While it's easy to get caught up in the challenge of impressing the interviewer with your brilliant answers, it's also important that you don't lose sight of your other goal—trying to determine whether this situation is right for you, whether this job is worthy of your talents and commitment.

With this in mind, here are a few key questions *I* would want to ask:

- Can you give me a formal, written description of the position? I'm interested in reviewing in detail the major activities involved and what results are expected.

- Does this job usually lead to other positions at the company? Which ones?

- Tell me some of the particular skills or attributes that you want in the candidate for this position?

- Please tell me a little bit about the people with whom I'll be working most closely.

- What do *you* like best about this company? Why?

- What is the company's ranking within the industry? Does this position represent a change from where it was a few years ago?

In addition to these, here's the most comprehensive list of questions I can devise:

Questions about the company

- What are its leading products or services? What products or services is it planning to introduce in the near future?

- What are its key markets? Are they growing?

- Will it be entering any new markets in the next couple of years? Which ones and via what kind of distribution channel(s)?

- What growth rate are you currently anticipating? Will this be accomplished internally or through acquisitions?

- Who owns it?

- Please tell me about your own tenure with the company.

- How many employees work for the organization? In how many offices? In this office?

- What has been its layoff history in the last five years? Do you anticipate any cutbacks in the near future and, if so, how will they impact my department or position?

- What major problems or challenges has it recently faced? How were they addressed? What results do you expect?

- What is its share of each of its markets?

- Which other companies serving those markets pose a serious threat?

- Please tell me more about your training programs. Do you offer reimbursement for job-related education? Time off?

- What is your hiring philosophy?
- What are its plans and prospects for growth and expansion?
- What are its goals in the next few years?

Questions about the department or division

- Explain the organizational structure of the department and its primary functions and responsibilities.
- To whom will I be reporting? To whom does he or she report?
- With which other departments does this department work most closely?
- How many people work exclusively in this department?
- What problems is this department facing? What are its current goals and objectives?

Questions about the job

- How many people will be reporting to me?
- Is relocation an option, a possibility, or a requirement?
- How did this job become available? Was the previous person promoted? What is their new title? Was the previous person fired? Why?
- Would I be able to speak with the person who held this job previously?

- Could you describe a typical day in this position?

- How long has this position been available?

- How many other candidates have you interviewed? How many more will you be interviewing before you make a decision?

- Is there no one from within the organization who is qualified for this position?

- Before you're able to reach a hiring decision, how many more interviews should I expect to go through and with whom?

- Where will I be working? May I see my office/cubicle/closet/floor mat?

- How advanced/current is the hardware and software I will be expected to use?

- How much day-to-day autonomy will I have?

Chapter 10

How to Deal With Illegal Questions

In an ideal world, companies and managers would judge their employees only on the basis of their job performance, and candidates would be measured only against a set of criteria deemed important for doing the job well.

Our world isn't ideal. In the *real* world, few people can judge others with pure objectivity. As a result, many managers and even entire companies and professions discriminate.

The most unpleasant manifestations of the real world for too many job candidates are questions and remarks related to sex, race, ethnic background, marital status, and all of the other ridiculous traits upon which the ignorant and sometimes not so ignorant think it fair to judge people.

What can you do if you come face to face with racism, sexism, or some other ugly "ism" during a job interview?

All too many candidates feel that they have to endure and answer politely every question an interviewer asks, no matter how distasteful or irrelevant.

That's pure nonsense. Candidates have rights. If the interviewer doesn't seem to know what these rights are, *you* should.

This chapter will explain your rights as an interviewee and what you can do if you feel an interviewer has acted inappropriately or unlawfully.

What does *that* have to do with my job?

It's pretty easy to tell when a question is inappropriate—it has little or nothing to do with how the candidate might perform on the job. And that's pretty much what the law states—interviewers can ask questions that have to do with job performance. When they ask questions that are unrelated to the work to be performed, they could be skating on thin ice.

Every state has fair-employment laws governing the screening of job candidates and lists of questions considered unlawful for employers to ask on job applications and during interviews. Check with your state's Fair Employment Practices Commission for more details.

In the meantime, here are some general guidelines to help you recognize discriminatory or otherwise illegal questions:

- **Name.** Sure, that seems innocent enough. Prospective employers will need to know your name to address you. But in many states, you are protected from questions that seek to determine your birth name if you've had it legally changed, or your maiden name if you're a married woman. However, employers *are* permitted to ask what other names they should check to determine your employment history.

- **Marital/family status.** Employers are not permitted to ask about your marital status or plans for marriage. Likewise, they are forbidden from asking women about their plans for having children. I think this is an area in which it is very easy, for women especially, to "open the door" to a host of questions you aren't required to answer—unless you bring them up. After all, what could seem more innocent than chit-chatting about your fiancé or spouse or kids? Do you really want to discuss your tentative plans for having a child within a year? Think about it.

♦ **Age.** Employers cannot ask for your birth date or about facts that might reveal your birth date, such as the year you graduated from high school.

♦ **Creed.** Under no circumstances is an employer permitted to ask about your religious affiliation or the religious holidays you observe. In addition, interviewers are not permitted to make even simple statements such as, "This is a Christian (or Jewish or Muslim) company," perhaps looking for some sort of reaction from you as a prospective employee.

♦ **Nationality.** Employers are generally forbidden to ask about your ancestry, descent, parentage, or nationality, that of your parents or spouse, or to inquire about your "mother tongue." Technically speaking, an interviewer could not ask, "Is that an Irish name?" but she *could* ask you what language(s) you speak or write. Companies are required to ask you for proof of citizenship or status as a resident, such as a green card, but only after you're hired.

- **Race.** Employers cannot ask you about the color of your skin or that of your relatives or spouse.

- **Sexual orientation.** Employers may not ask if you're straight, gay, or bisexual.

- **Military service.** The employer can ask how long and in what branch of the service you were in, but not the type of discharge you received.

- **Physical condition.** The 1992 Americans With Disabilities Act (ADA) precludes employers from asking about diseases for which you've been treated, whether you've ever been hospitalized, if you've ever filed for worker's compensation, and if you are taking any medication.

  While they cannot ask something like, "Do you have any physical disabilities?" they certainly can ask, "Are you able to perform the job for which you're applying, either with or without an accommodation?"

- **Photograph.** Employers are not permitted to ask for photographs to be attached to job applications.

- **Organizations.** Employers can ask about your membership in organizations that *you* consider important to the performance of the job. Otherwise, this can be another sneaky way to find out about religion (if you're a member of B'nai B'rith or the Christian Church Fellowship, for example), race (if you're a member of the NAACP and it's not obvious you are African-American), political affiliation, etc.

- **Other personal questions.** Employers may not ask about your overall financial situation—outside income, debts, your credit rating, whether you own a home, or if you've gone bankrupt. Unless you're applying for a position in law enforcement, most employers are not entitled to know if you've been arrested, unless the arrest resulted in a conviction. Nevertheless, in some states, employers can only ask about felony convictions, not misdemeanors.

How to react when you're asked a "wrong" question

Despite a plethora of lawsuits charging employers with discriminatory hiring practices, unlawful questions still are commonly asked during interviews. This is particularly true of interviews by hiring managers, who generally have not received the extensive education on legal issues human resource professionals now routinely undergo.

What do you do if you're asked a question that you believe to be unlawful? You have three choices:

1. Refuse, on principle, to answer any unlawful question, even if you'd come up smelling like a rose anyway.

2. Be a pragmatist—provide any answers you feel wouldn't hurt you, while tactfully sidestepping those that could.

3. Use a mixture of both approaches.

Let's say you have an "obviously" Italian last name, like Rutigliano. You greet the interviewer and he says, "Boy, that's Italian, isn't it?" You should smile politely and not answer at all. It's quite possible he meant absolutely no offense. However, if later the interviewer pursues the line of questioning with, "Were

your parents born in the United States or on the other side?"
you can dodge it one more time by saying something like, "They
don't remember. They were just little babies." But by now you
should be wary of any further signs of prejudice or insensitivity.
If the interviewer still doesn't get the hint, and continues to allude
to your heritage, then you should point out to him that he is doing
something illegal. You might say, "I really don't see what my
ancestry has to do with my application for this job. You must
know that you're not supposed to ask me questions like this."

Believe it or not, you could still stay on the interviewer's
good side if you handle the situation in a diplomatic way. At the
same time, you will have put him on notice that you are aware
of the law and do not take it as lightly as he obviously does. You
also have told him that he has opened himself up to a discrimination charge.

Such a line of questioning, however, might well indicate
that you don't want to work for this supervisor under any circumstances. He's obviously an ignorant, insensitive person.

Harassment: A problem that won't go away

Talk to any employment lawyer and she will tell you that
sexual discrimination cases are the largest part of her practice. As more multimillion-dollar settlements are being won
against companies that allow sexual harassment to continue,
more and more employers are beginning to see the issue as a
potential powder keg—and ordering up training programs to
discourage it.

Despite all of this, however, sexual harassment still exists
in the workplace—and the interviewing office.

Women have told us about being asked to dinner during interviews with male hiring managers. Others talked about interviewers staring at their chests throughout the interview.

What are you to do if this happens? Well, unfortunately, the best choice is to do nothing—bring the interview to a close as quickly as possible and scratch the position off your list. Then follow up with the human resources department and report the interviewer's behavior.

If you still want to work at that company, ask about positions in other departments. If you encounter this kind of discrimination in your interview with the human resources department, scratch the company off your list altogether. You would undoubtedly be walking into a work situation that is very uncomfortable.

Married with children?

Even when sex is not the issue, *your* sex still might be. Some employers still have the nerve to ask women about their marital or familial status. Many supervisors don't want to offer a position to a woman who they think is going to get pregnant and leave them in a few months.

Your best bet is to meet such questions head on. Your marital status and family plans are simply none of your prospective employer's business. Make this a non-issue by talking about such things as your excellent attendance record and the need you see for a healthy balance in your life.

If the interviewer pursues this line of questioning, remind him that your husband (or lack of one) and family (or lack of one) are not what you came to his office to discuss—that you are interested in committing yourself to the job he has open or you wouldn't have shown up for the interview.

Remember, too, that many interviewers are aware of the laws surrounding questions about sex, sexual orientation, and family status. However, all bets are off when the interviewee introduces the material into the interview situation.

For instance, a female acquaintance of mine, Karen, interviewed at one of the largest companies in the country. The skilled interviewer kept shifting gears between very job-related and very personal questions.

Although Karen was a savvy interviewee and had little trouble deflecting the questions she knew to be inappropriate, she let her guard down once, beginning an answer with "My husband..."

The interviewer pounced on that as quickly as a salesman can get his foot in an open door. She began asking questions about what Karen's husband did and how he "felt about his wife having a job that required a lot of travel."

The interviewer apparently wanted to know what Karen's career and family plans were, but knew better than to come right out and ask such unlawful questions.

Once *Karen* introduced the subject of her husband, however, the interviewer felt her family life was fair game. She couldn't ask anything as obviously unlawful as, "Are you married?" or "Don't you want to have children, and won't your career interfere with that?" But she still wanted to know the answers to those questions.

I must reiterate that you should never bring up personal material yourself unless you're willing to answer questions about it. Savvy interviewers will grab at any opportunity to get information they want without running the risk of ending up in court. Their defense will be, "*I* never asked about her family. *She* brought it up." And while it still might not be entirely on the "up and up," it may well prove enough of a defense.

What to do after the fact

If you are not offered a position after being asked unlawful questions, you might have grounds for charging the employer with discrimination. The interviewer asked non-job-related questions, and you have reason to believe that your refusal to answer these questions or the answers you provided led to your not being hired.

The operative word here is "might." You would have to prove that the questions were asked for the purpose of discriminating among applicants for an illegal reason.

For instance, if the manager asking all those questions about Italian ancestry subsequently hired another Italian, you wouldn't have much of a claim, despite the fact that you were asked illegal questions.

If you *do* think that you have grounds for a charge of discrimination, you should file your charges simultaneously with the appropriate state agency and the Equal Employment Opportunity Commission (EEOC). The EEOC generally will wait until the state agency has conducted an investigation, then conduct an investigation of its own.

As you might expect when dealing with government agencies, you might not hear anything for years. When the EEOC does act, it may be solely to determine whether there is reason to believe your charge is true. Therefore, if you are anxious for justice, you should request that the EEOC issue you a notice to sue 180 days after you file your charge.

If you are right

If the EEOC determines in your favor, it will attempt to mediate the dispute between you and the employer. Failing to arrange for such an agreement, the Commission will either file a suit or issue you a letter giving you the right to sue the employer. You must file your suit within 90 days of receiving such a letter.

Even if you go through all this trouble and win your lawsuit, don't expect to receive a colossal settlement. The most you'll probably get from the employer for an interview "indiscretion" is the equivalent of about one year's salary.

As I've stressed throughout this book, the primary thing to remember about interviews is that you are there as a participant, not as a powerless victim.

If you feel that the interviewer is asking you questions that shouldn't be asked, the first step is to try to shrug them off and change the direction of the conversation.

The next step is to inform the employer that you know he or she is doing something unlawful. This should put any interviewer on warning that you won't submit to illegal interview behavior, or the discrimination that might result from it, without a fight.

The last step is to terminate the interview and, possibly, seek to bring formal charges against the company and the interviewer.

My own legal disclaimer

I am not an attorney, and nothing in this chapter should be taken as legal advice. If you feel a prospective employer is guilty of discrimination, your first step should be to contact the appropriate government agencies, as well as an attorney to accurately assess your rights and options under federal law and the laws and regulations in your state and industry.

Tips for fending off illegal questions

- **Know your rights.** Do some research to find out what questions are out of bounds in your particular state, industry, or profession.

- **Don't open the door for the interviewer.** That is, don't bring up subjects you don't want to talk about. If you do, the interviewer is likely to ask what would otherwise have been illegal questions—if *you* hadn't opened the door first.

- **Change the subject.** If you feel that the interviewer is asking you questions that shouldn't be asked, the first step is to try to shrug them off and change the direction of the conversation.

- **Give him the benefit of the doubt.** After all, you are here because you want the job. So it's up to you to weigh your personal reactions to certain searching questions against your desire to have this job. Many hiring managers may not realize they are in the wrong. Give them the benefit of the doubt.

- **Warn the interviewer—subtly.** Tell the interviewer in a non-threatening way that you know the questions she is asking are inappropriate. This should deliver the message that you know your rights and aren't willing to be a victim of discrimination.

- **End the interview.** If the interviewer refuses to back off, end the interview quickly. After all, would you really want to work at a company or for a person capable of such narrow-minded attitudes? If you think you have a strong case, look into bringing formal charges against the company and the interviewer.

Chapter 11

How to Follow Up Your Interviews

Yogi Berra said many memorable things, most of them head-scratchers, but none as famous as the line, "It ain't over 'til it's over." If the interview is to prove meaningful for you and you want to increase your chances of landing that job—even if you're utterly sure that you knocked the interviewer's socks off—don't presume the interview is over when you leave your would-be employer's office.

To increase your chances of landing that job, you must take several follow-up steps.

Don't be just another candidate

I hope you learn at least one great lesson from every boss you have during your career. One of my most memorable bosses taught me several lessons that I find myself applying at least once every week.

The single most valuable lesson he taught me was that the world is full of mediocre people. It is, therefore, relatively easy (he asserted) to be perceived as excellent—so easy that it makes no sense *not* to take steps to rise above the crowd.

The important thing to remember is to *act promptly*. When you meet someone who might be important to you (such as your interviewer), write her a letter and see that it's mailed that very day. Think how great you'll look next to others who said that they'd contact that person and never did—or did so *weeks* later.

Take my word for it—that's great advice. On the day of your interview, use it. Do not pass "Go." Proceed directly to your computer or typewriter, type a letter (or an e-mail) to the person who interviewed you and walk it to the mailbox.

The letter should express your gratitude for the chance to be considered for the position. It should, like the initial cover letter you sent, emphasize one of your key strengths. It should also mention something you or the interviewer said.

Most importantly, the follow-up letter should let the "real you" show through. After all, you are now writing to someone you've met and who, presumably, has gotten to know you pretty well. There's a good example of a follow-up letter on page 168.

Touting your references

If the interviewer asks for a list of references, tell him you will get back with a list that afternoon or, if it the interview ends late in the day, the following morning.

Does this make you seem unprepared? Shouldn't you go into the interview with the list? After all, your resume says, "References available upon request," and here's the request.

Well, in the world of interviews, stalling for a little time before giving the references is SOP (standard operating procedure).

The reason you want to wait is to forewarn your prospective references that a call might be coming from Mr. Somebody of ABC Corporation. If they are going to give you a good reference, they should be prepared. And if they're not, you'll want to change the list—fast.

You've worked too hard to get this job to let a reference check blow it for you. That means you should manage your references as well as you've managed every other part of the interview.

The first step is to line them up *before* going on your first interview. Speak to all of the people you'll be including on your list, and let each one know how you will be presenting yourself and what exactly you'll be saying about your affiliation with him or her.

It's a good idea to follow up these conversations with a letter and a copy of your resume. This will allow your reference to see just how you're presenting your job, internship, or independent course work. Your resume will also tell him or her what you are saying about your abilities and accomplishments.

Unsure about what one of these references might say about you? Ask. If you feel that he or she remembers your relationship differently than you do, resolve the situation.

What they won't say

In these litigious times, many references are afraid to say anything about a past associate for fear of being sued for libel or slander. Therefore, you should be aware of the things that your references *won't* say.

If you know that a reference will offer only the bare facts—date of employment and job title—try your best to leave her off the list. Employers might read unwillingness to say anything as merely avoidance of saying anything bad.

But no matter how careful you are at this stage of the process, there's a chance that the manager or professor with an unfavorable opinion of you will be contacted. If you think this might damage your chances of securing the job you covet, do your best to score a preemptive strike.

Tell the hiring manager or human resources department why you might receive an unfavorable reference from that manager. One of the most common and easily accepted reasons for a bad reference is the vague "personality conflict." Indicate that you and the manager did not get along, but that there are other people at the organization who can vouch for the quality of your work. Give one or more of their names.

Once again, follow up

It's a good idea to follow up with your references to see if they were called and, if they were, ask how the questioning went. What were some of the things that your prospective employer wanted to know? Is it obvious from their questions that one particular area of your background is troubling them?

If that's the case, you might be able to overcome their objections with a follow-up phone call a week to 10 days after the interview.

It's perfectly acceptable for you to inquire about the status of the position. Have they filled it? Do they expect to reach a decision in the near future? When? Are you still in the running?

This phone call will give the interviewer an opportunity to ask you about anything he heard during the reference check that is bothering him.

What if you change your mind?

Did something during the interview make you decide that you *didn't* want to work at the company? Then politely take yourself out of the running. Write a letter to the screening interviewer and the hiring manager indicating that have decided to pursue other options. An example is on page 171.

Following up in a professional manner will leave your interviewers with a positive impression, so they will be less likely to label you "unreliable," "indecisive," or worse. You never know: Someday you might decide that company is perfect for you.

Remember: Write a thank-you letter on the day of your interview, follow up with your references, and respond immediately to the interviewer's requests for more information.

Your prompt attention to these matters is sure to help you stand out from the crowd of candidates. And it will serve as just one more indication of what a terrific, timely employee you will be.

If you get the job, write a letter either accepting it (see page 169) or rejecting it. And if they reject you, write a letter that may well set you up for another job in the future (see page 170).

Finishing touches

- **Nourish your network.** If a colleague or former associate referred you to the company or arranged a personal introduction with the interviewer or hiring manager, be sure to drop that person a note of thanks as well.

- **Replay the highs—and the lows.** What went well during the interviewing process? What could you have done better? The point is not to berate yourself for what you did or didn't say. You merely want to make sure you keep doing the things that worked—and working on what didn't—so you can ace your next interview.

- **Rewrite your resume.** Did the interviewer have any questions that you could clarify through your resume? Did you find yourself talking about accomplishments you forgot to include? If so, now is the time to revise your resume—before you send it out again.

- **Keep in touch.** The hiring process can move at a snail's pace in corporate America. Often, the larger the corporation, the slower the pace. So don't panic if a week or two passes before you hear anything. No news may be good news. If time stretches on, it's okay to call to find out if the job has been filled. Use the opportunity to remind the employer of your interest and qualifications.

- **Accept—in your own time and on your own terms.** Never accept an offer at the time it is tendered. Take a day or two to think about it. Tell the interviewer when you will announce your decision. If you do decide to refuse the offer, politely tell the employer why you don't feel you can accept the position.

◆ **Congratulate yourself.** You made it through one of life's more stressful experiences with flying colors. You've proven you're a real pro. Now you're on your way.

AFTER A JOB INTERVIEW

1497 Lilac Street
Worcester, MA 01602
October 5, 2002
222-555-3434
E-mail: HALT@loa.reg

Ms. Ellen Selver
Director of Human Resources
Distinguished Fidelity
175 Boylston Avenue
Boston, MA 01949

Dear Ms. Selver:
Thank you for the opportunity to interview yesterday for the analyst trainee position. I enjoyed meeting you and John Fitzgerald and learning more about Distinguished Fidelity.

Your organization appears to be growing in a direction that parallels my interests and career goals. The interview with you and your staff confirmed my initial positive impressions of Distinguished Fidelity, and I want to reiterate my strong interest in working for you. My prior experience as treasurer of my class, plus my Business College training in accounting and finance would enable me to progress steadily through your training program and become a productive member of your research team.

Again, thank you for your consideration. If you need any additional information from me, please feel free to call.

Yours truly,

David Halter

cc: Mr. John Fitzgerald

ACCEPTING A JOB OFFER

1497 Lilac Street
Worcester, MA 01602
October 5, 2002
222-555-3434
E-mail: HALT@loa.reg

Ms. Ellen Selver
Director of Human Resources
Distinguished Fidelity
175 Boylston Avenue
Boston, MA 01949

Dear Ms. Selver:

I want to thank you and Mr. Fitzgerald for giving me the opportunity to work for Distinguished Fidelity. I am very pleased to accept the position as an analyst trainee with your Investment Unit. The position entails exactly the kind of work I want to do, and I know that I will do a good job for you.

As we discussed, I shall begin work on Dec. 1, 2001. In the interim I shall complete all the necessary employment forms, obtain the required physical examination and locate housing. I plan to be in Boston within the next two weeks and would like to deliver the paperwork to you personally. At that time, we could handle any remaining items pertaining to my employment. I'll call next week to schedule an appointment with you.

Sincerely yours,

David Halter

cc: Mr. John Fitzgerald

IN RESPONSE TO REJECTION

1497 Lilac Street
Worcester, MA 01602
October 5, 2002
222-555-3434
E-mail: HALT@loa.reg

Ms. Ellen Selver
Director of Human Resources
Distinguished Fidelity
175 Boylston Avenue
Boston, MA 01949

Dear Ms. Selver:

Thank you for giving me the opportunity to interview for the analyst trainee position. I appreciate your consideration and interest in me.

Although I am disappointed in not being selected for your current vacancy, I want you to know that I appreciated the courtesy and professionalism shown to me during the entire selection process. I enjoyed meeting you, John Fitzgerald, and the other members of your research staff. My meetings confirmed that Distinguished Fidelity would be an exciting place to work and build a career.

I want to reiterate my strong interest in working for you. Please keep me in mind if a similar position becomes available in the near future.

Again, thank you for the opportunity to interview and best wishes to you and your staff.

Sincerely yours,

David Halter

cc: Mr. John Fitzgerald

WITHDRAWING FROM CONSIDERATION

1497 Lilac Street
Worcester, MA 01602
December 5, 2002
222-555-3434
E-mail: HALT@loa.reg

Ms. Ellen Selver
Distinguished Fidelity
175 Boylston Avenue
Boston, MA 01949

Dear Ms. Selver:

It was indeed a pleasure meeting with you and Mr. Fitzgerald last week to discuss your needs for an analyst trainee.

As I discussed with you during our meetings, I believe one purpose of preliminary interviews is to explore areas of mutual interest and to assess the fit between the individual and the position. After careful consideration, I have decided to withdraw from consideration for the position.

My decision is based upon two factors. First, the emphasis on data entry is certainly needed in your case, but I would prefer more balance in my work activities. Second, the position would require more travel than I am willing to accept with my other responsibilities.

I want to thank you for interviewing me and giving me the opportunity to learn about your needs. You have a fine staff and I would have enjoyed working with them.

Yours truly,

David Halter

cc: Mr. John Fitzgerald

Chapter 12

How to Negotiate Your First Salary

There are many schools of thought about how to handle the discussion of salary during job interviews. Some experts advise bringing the topic to a head as soon as possible. Others suggest avoiding the subject entirely, as if getting a paycheck were some unspeakable practice.

Common sense dictates a course somewhere between these two extremes. I recommend that you avoid bringing up the subject of salary yourself during your screening and selection interviews. If the interviewer brings it up, answer her questions. But it's really in your best interest to avoid getting down to the brass tacks of salary negotiation *until an offer has been made.*

The interview is a classic buy-sell situation. You are trying to sell yourself to a company and get the best price you can. The company is making sure that it wants to buy what you're offering, and, naturally, hopes to pay as little as you'll accept.

Not talking about price in a situation like this is ludicrous. But talking about it at the wrong time is foolish. Timing is everything in life. *You have nothing to gain by discussing dollars and cents before you've convinced the employer that you're the right person for the job. In other words, the best time to discuss salary is* after *you get the offer.*

Most likely you won't find yourself in a bidding war. Just getting out of college, you'll be applying for entry-level positions that have relatively narrow salary ranges. What's more, you don't really have that much to sell yet, and the competition is fiercer than it's been in a while.

Nevertheless, you are not a commodity. If you can stand apart from the crowd of applicants, if you can convince the employer that an extra couple of thousand dollars would be well-spent on a dynamo like you, then one of the only sure ways *not* to get it is by putting a price tag around your neck too early in the proceedings.

In Chapter 8, I stressed that showing an interest in the interviewer is critically important. Trying to speak about something—salary—that he has no *desire* to speak about until he finishes asking questions is one sure way to make the interviewer feel that you are self-absorbed and uninterested in anything but money.

Would you buy something from a salesperson who only wanted to impress upon you how much something cost?

Of course not.

Why would a company hire someone only interested in seeing how much he could get?

I, and most experienced hiring managers I know, have at least one story about candidates who ask only about salary, benefits, and days off. None of these subjects is a good one to ask about when the employer first asks you if you have any questions!

What if the interviewer blinks first?

You can always tell when an interviewer is paying people too little. This kind of interviewer will bring up salary early on to determine whether she can afford you before spending the time to interview you.

Okay, that might not always be the reason that the subject of salary is broached too early. It might just be that the interviewer is inexperienced or has a premonition that you'll want more than he can afford to pay.

Whatever the reason, if the subject of salary *does* come up too early, sidestep it. Remember: It can't possibly do you any good to discuss salary before you've sold the employer. So, handle the question as you would some of the sensitive questions we discussed at the beginning of Chapter 10— diplomatically avoid them. One of the following replies might prove useful:

- ◆ "I have an idea of the salary range for the position from your ad (or from what the recruiter said). It sounds like a reasonable range to me."

- ◆ "I'm willing to consider any reasonable salary offer."

- ◆ "I'd like to hear a little more about what my responsibilities will be before I can feel comfortable about talking about a starting salary."

- ◆ "From what I know about the position and the company, I don't think we'll have any trouble agreeing on a fair salary."

- ◆ "I'm well aware of what starting salaries are for this position within the industry. I'm sure that if salaries here are comparable, we'll have no trouble coming to an agreement."

Remember, you *don't* want to talk about money even though the employer brought it up. Defer, defer, defer the discussion until later.

Fielding the offer

So, you're an ace candidate. You have impressed the interviewer so much so that a couple of days later you get an offer by phone.

You're delirious. You want to shout with joy. After all, you've sold a stranger on yourself—that's a terrific vote of confidence. You got the job!

Don't get too carried away just yet. You've captured the high ground in your search for a job. Now you want to take advantage of that.

Earlier in the chapter, I stressed that the interview is a buy-sell situation. Now that the company is sold on you, *you're* the one who must make the decision to buy.

Take your time. You should never—repeat, *never*—accept a job the minute it's offered to you. Even though you've probably thought about little else since your last interview with the employer, and have thoroughly made up your mind that you will accept the job if it's offered, tell the company that you "need some time to consider it."

You could say you want to sleep on it, or think about it over the weekend, or talk it over with your spouse or "adviser."

Most companies will push you for a fairly quick response— they have probably interviewed other promising candidates for the position and don't want to lose them if their leading candidate turns them down.

However, don't act before *you're* ready to. Tell the person making the offer that you need a short time to think it over, thank him or her profusely for thinking so highly of you and agree on a day and a time that you'll call back with your answer.

This will give you time to consider the reality of the offer—including the fact that you will be working at the company for (hopefully) quite some time.

If the offer stinks

Most often, college graduates entering the job market will be interviewing for positions with a narrow salary range—$16,000 to $18,000, $24,000 to $27,000, etc.— depending on the profession and industry.

If you are offered a salary close to the top of that range—$17,500 or $26,000 in the above examples—consider it a compliment and don't think too hard about pushing for more money. You don't have that much to gain anyway—particularly in today's performance-based job market.

But if you're offered a salary at the floor of the range, push for some more money. Tell the interviewer, "I understood that the position was paying as much as $24,000, and yet you're offering me only $21,500. You told me that you've interviewed several candidates for the position. Well, you've selected me because of my academic record and the drive I've demonstrated in securing top internships. Therefore, I believe a salary of at least $24,000 is reasonable for me to expect."

This will usually encourage the interviewer to raise his offer a bit, though he might have been saving the top end for people with more advanced degrees or some experience in the field (despite what the ad said).

If you're still leaning toward the position, ask when you will receive your first salary review. If the answer is on your anniversary date, see if you can push for an earlier review to make up some of the shortfall between the offer and your expectations.

Tell the person making the offer, "I am very flattered by the offer and I wish we could agree on a higher salary. Could you give me my first salary review in, say, six months, rather than 12?"

This is a rather easy concession for the interviewer to make. He will think that he is getting the candidate he wants for only half the difference between what you want to earn and what he wants to pay.

If you can't pay the rent

This might be a case of closing the barn door after the cow has escaped.

But if you are very surprised at the low salary offers you are getting during your first interviews, then you're, to quote former President George Bush, "in deep doo doo."

As you prepare to embark on a career, you should make sure that it is one that will fulfill your needs. And if a high salary is one of them, you'd better be aiming for a profession or technical discipline. If you expect to get $50,000 a year (or $30,000, for that matter) in your first job in, say, publishing, you're in for a rude awakening.

Before you go on your first interview, you should have gained, through your research, a pretty good idea of the numbers employers will be discussing with you when the question of salary comes up. If you're shocked the first time salary comes up during an interview, you are in for a bumpy ride on your way to your first job.

Consider the whole picture

I would encourage you also to look at the entire value of the compensation package. Some companies provide very generous benefits packages—including stock options, unlimited dental care, even company cars and free lunches along with "standard" health insurance and vacation days. If these benefits don't immediately add to your bottom line, at least you won't have to pay for them out of your own pocket.

Most company vacation policies are fairly standard: two weeks for the first three years, three weeks thereafter. Some companies offer "comp" time in exchange for a great deal of overtime. Some match employee deposits to retirement plans. Some require employees to contribute something toward health insurance. A number of benefits—such as profit sharing—may not be immediately available to you.

You should have learned something about the company's standard benefits package early in the game. If, at this stage, you find the offer abysmal, why are you still considering that company?

If there are any other questions you feel will affect your decision about whether to accept this job, you had better ask them now, while you are still considering the offer!

Remember, it ain't over till it's over

After all this work, I'm assuming you finally accepted an offer—somewhere! And that they're even going to pay you to show up. Breathe a sigh of relief and experience the thrill of victory in this tough job market.

However, this is hardly the time to relax and forget about all of the skills that helped you land this swell job.

Start off on the right foot by writing a letter to your new manager, telling him how much you're looking forward to "opening day" at your new company.

And don't forget to drop a line to your references and all of the other people in your network. Tell them where you've landed and how grateful you are to them for their contribution to the effort. These contacts will prove helpful to you—perhaps even on your new job. They are sure to grow more valuable over time, however, in the increasingly likely event that you soon end up in the market for a new position.

Once you start your new position, you'll be expected to live up to all of those wonderful things you said about yourself during the job interview. I'm sure that if you followed the suggestions in this book, particularly the advice on getting to know yourself, you'll do well in your first job—and during the entire course of your career.

Good luck!

Tips on wrapping up a winning "package"

◆ **Wait until you receive an offer.** Defer any question of salary that comes up early in the interview with an answer like this: "Colleen in human resources indicated the salary range for this position, and it seems about right to me." Or , "I'd like to know a little bit more about the job responsibilities and the level of expertise you're expecting before I feel comfortable discussing a salary."

◆ **Know your worth.** Remember that the company wants you. They have decided you are the best candidate they have met. This puts you in a position of power. If they balk at your initial salary demand, remind them of a few specific benefits they stand to gain from hiring you.

◆ **Research compensation levels.** Look within your industry and locally—within your city and state. If you don't already know the salary range for the specific position you're considering, find out. You need to go into salary negotiations armed with this information.

◆ **Negotiate the perks.** Make sure you understand the value of all the potential benefits in the salary/benefits package. Benefits can vary widely. Some companies buy employees company cars and club memberships. Others give bonuses or extra time off.

- **Go for the top.** If that is more than the company will pay, the interviewer will counter with another offer. Work toward a compromise from there.

- **Get it in writing.** Especially if you negotiate a complex, nonstandard salary/benefits package. Be sure you have something in writing—either a letter or memo from the employer, or one you've sent that's been accepted—before you give notice to your current employer.

Index

A

accepting a job offer, letter sample, 169

Activities Data Input Sheet, 30

answering questions accurately, 119-120

Awards & Honors Data Input Sheet, 31

B

body language, 94-96, 105

C

calls, receiving positive, 56-57

campus recruiters, 47

changes you'd make, questions about, 130-131

College Data Input Sheet, 28

college grads, tips for, 123-124

comfortable, becoming, 14

company information, obtaining, 42-46

company,
   learning about the, 35-36
   questions about the, 145-146

H

harassment, 154-155

High School Data Input
Sheet, 26

hiring manager,
interview with a, 101-112
targeting the, 52

honest, being, 105

honors and awards, 19

human resources, 52, 54

I

illegal questions, 149-159
tips for fending off, 159

informational interview, 66
goals of, 66-67

informational interview,
preparing for an, 69-72
setting up an, 68-69

in-person screening
interview, 82-83

internships and part-time
work, 132-133

interview as an adventure,
104

interview don'ts, 96-97

interview follow-up, 161-171

interview process, 14

interview questions,
answering, 125-147

interview technique, 113-124

interview types, 77-89

interview,
after the, 72-73
getting an, 51-60
what to expect during your,
77-90

interviewer, finding out about
the, 47-48

interviewing for information,
66

J

job, questions about the,
146-147

K

knowing yourself better,
14-15

L

Language Data Input Sheet,
33

languages, fluency in, 20

learning more during the
interview, 48-49